Contents

AA309 B2
Arts: Level 3

CULTURE, IDENTITY AND POWER IN THE ROMAN EMPIRE

BLOCK TWO

Rome, Italy and the Empire

Prepared for the Course Team by Valerie Hope (Block Convenor), Chris Emlyn-Jones, Paula James and Phil Perkins

The Open University
Walton Hall, Milton Keynes MK7 6AA

First published 2000. Second edition 2002.

Edited, designed and typeset by The Open University

Printed and bound in the United Kingdom by the Alden Group, Oxford

This text is a component of the Open University course AA309 *Culture, Identity and Power in the Roman Empire.* Details of this and other Open University courses can be obtained from the Course Reservations Centre, PO Box 724, The Open University, Milton Keynes MK7 6ZS, United Kingdom: tel. (00 44) (0)1908 653231.

For availability of this or other course components, contact Open University Worldwide Ltd, The Berrill Building, Walton Hall, Milton Keynes MK7 6AA, United Kingdom: tel. (00 44) (0)1908 858585, fax (00 44) (0)1908 858787, e-mail ouwenq@open.ac.uk

Alternatively, much useful course information can be obtained from the Open University's website http://www.open.ac.uk

ISBN 0 7492 8592 3

23913B/aa309block2i2.1

Introduction

In this block you will consider the relationship between Rome and Italy and also the impact of the empire on both the city of Rome and the Italian peninsula. The block will raise issues fundamental to the central themes of the course. How did the power and might of Rome impinge on the cities of Italy, undermining or altering their culture and identity? You will take a look at the so-called process of Romanization – the adoption of Roman customs and traditions by non-Roman populations – which is not a concept derived from the Romans themselves but a term coined by modern scholars to summarize the cultural imperialism of Roman rule (look back at Essay One for further discussion). As you work through this block, and indeed the subsequent blocks, you should keep this term in mind. How appropriate is it? In particular, you will need to consider the difficulty of defining, in precise terms, the nature of both Roman culture and Roman identity. Remember, for example, the points raised in Essay Three about the cosmopolitan nature of the city of Rome. Rome may have created and headed the empire, but in the process Rome itself was influenced and changed. Cultural exchange rather than cultural imperialism may be a more appropriate way of defining the relationship between Rome and the provinces.

To explore these issues in relation to Rome and Italy you will focus on certain key topics: how the relationship between Rome and Italy was described in literature, the influence on the Roman character of provincial wealth, and the economic impact on Italy of the acquisition of the empire. In addition you will consider two Italian towns in detail from the perspectives of architecture, the inhabitants and the economy to assess the degree to which Rome impacted on these settlements.

The work in this block will draw on diverse types of evidence. Some of these, such as poetry, monumental architecture and statues, will be familiar from Block One and the skills developed there will be practised here. In addition, in this block you will be introduced to the techniques of reading archaeological site plans, to the conventions and content of Latin inscriptions and to the significance and function of portraiture.

This block is divided into three parts. Part One introduces the relationship between Rome and Italy and should take approximately half a week's study time. Parts Two and Three, which focus on the Italian towns of Ostia and Pompeii and explore the impact of the empire on Italy, each involve just under two weeks' study time.

Part One: Rulers and ruled – Rome and Italy

BY VALERIE HOPE AND PHIL PERKINS

In this first part of the block you will explore briefly the expansion of Roman power into Italy and one of the methods – colonization – by which Rome's influence was maintained. You will also begin to consider the impact of Roman culture on the cities of Italy, especially during the late republic.

1.1 Historical background

Italy was an area of the Roman empire like no other. By the first century AD Italy was perceived not so much as a province but as the Roman homeland; Rome and Italy were in many respects seen as synonymous. This, however, had not always been the case. This section provides a brief summary of Rome's early contact with Italy. To introduce the nature of the relationship between Rome and Italy you will also be asked to read a passage from Goodman.

Rome became the head of Italy through a process of conflict and alliance, and by 264 BC was the dominant political and military power in Italy. Italy was united as a confederacy; Rome had established alliances with the major cities and territories and created bonds of loyalty by founding colonies (see section 1.2). With the support of these Italian allies Rome could play a part on the world stage. It was interests in southern Italy that first brought Rome into conflict with the Carthaginians, who were the major power in the western Mediterranean. The claims of Rome and Carthage coincided in the island of Sicily, which led to the First Punic War (264–241 BC). Rome was victorious and Sicily became the first province of Rome. Through the Second Punic War (218–202 BC) Rome gained territory in Spain. The acquisition of an empire had begun.

The empire expanded with the support of Italy, but it was a Roman empire not an Italian one. The Italian cities were allied to Rome but the alliance was not equal in terms of power, influence and the benefits of empire. By the end of the second century BC some of the Italian allies were becoming increasingly discontented with their position in relation to Rome. The majority of the allies did not hold Roman citizenship and thus had little political voice. Yet the burden of military service fell on the Italians, while they received only limited economic and prestige benefits for it. The tensions eventually led to a conflict termed the Social War (from the Latin *socius*, meaning comrade or ally). The allies wanted social and political equality; they wanted not just citizenship but the advantages of empire and when Rome denied them these the allies fought for independence. The conflict was a long one (91–87 BC) and Rome eventually emerged as victor, but only after granting the concession of citizenship as a means of winning over the discontented allies. This grant of citizenship ultimately led to the political unification of Italy. Rome ceased to be a city state and became a state which embraced the whole of Italy: 'Rome was now Italy and Italy Rome' (Beard and Crawford, 1989, p.3).

To speak of 'Italy' during the middle and late years of the republic is in some ways misleading. Italy was not a country or an area that was politically united or linked by a common ethnic identity. The Social War saw the uniting of forces against a shared enemy, but not the creation of a definitive Italian national identity. In fact the term 'Italia' was not widely used before the Augustan period. Regional variations within the Italian peninsula in terms of origins, language and culture were considerable and it is interesting to explore the extent to which these perished or persisted after political unification. The power and influence of Rome may have been substantial, but did all places become but a pale imitation of the capital city?

Exercise

You should now read Goodman, pages 190–5 'Italy', in which he explores the impact of Rome on the cities of Italy. What does Goodman argue happened to the different peoples and communities under Roman rule?

Before reading you should note that the final two pages of this section of Goodman (pp.194–5) go on to describe economic impacts. We will not expand on this area here, but these pages will complete the picture and be useful for future reference.

Discussion

Note how Goodman says: 'The history of Italy in the early principate, then, is a story of the continuing disappearance of local cultural differences' (p.190). Goodman goes on to note that the cultures of Italy were diverse and did not immediately disappear. Italy was populated by people who traced their origins from, for example, Greeks, Etruscans, Celts and Samnites. Nevertheless, the force of Goodman's argument is clear – Italy became Romanized, with the loss of regional cultures and identities. Local languages were displaced by

> Latin, distinctive naming practices disappeared, the construction of unique funerary monuments declined and cities were greatly influenced by the influx of outside peoples. Everywhere presented a Roman face to the world. From the middle of page 193, however, there is a slight change of emphasis in Goodman's argument. He acknowledges that local law may have continued and notes in particular the continuing influence of Greek culture in certain Italian cities. Romanization was not a uniform process.

On the whole it may be that Goodman exaggerates or at least oversimplifies the influence of Rome on Italy during the late republic and early empire. This is not to deny the substantial changes which were afoot and the central role of Rome. But local identity may not have been completely subsumed to Roman identity. It was possible to be a Roman citizen while still regarding yourself as a citizen of your native town or city. Regional culture and identity persisted even if in a watered-down form. So much of both the available evidence and historical analysis is centred on Rome that it is easy to lose sight of local individuality. Also, did influence flow in only one direction? If we are to speak of the Romanization of Italy we may also need at least to consider the possibility of the 'Italianization' of Rome (Crawford, 1991, p.13). These issues of identity and its definition are ones that you should keep in mind as your work in this block progresses.

1.2 Citizenship and colonization in Cisalpine Gaul

In the previous section you looked at the expansion of Rome and the creation of Italy; now you will study this process in action by considering how a neighbouring area was annexed, incorporated into Italy and made 'Roman'. In this section you will be studying some aspects of the province of Cisalpine Gaul (Gallia Cisalpina, literally 'Gaul this side of the Alps'). It was the northern part of modern Italy, between the Alps and the Apennines, spanning the Po valley (Plate 2.1). This area became a Roman province when the Celtic tribes who lived there were conquered in 225–222 BC. Following this extension of Roman power the province was organized by constructing a road, the Via Aemilia, which ran from Rimini along the foothills of the Apennines. New Roman cities, with colonies of Roman citizens, were built at Piacenza, Cremona and Mantova in 218 BC to act as centres of political and military control. The early years of the province were turbulent, with Gallic resistance to Roman colonization and an alliance between the Gauls and Hannibal when he invaded Italy in the Second Punic War. Nevertheless, by the time of Augustus the continued creation of new cities had led to the spread and development of Roman ways of living.

In 25 and 15 BC the area of the province was enlarged by the conquest of neighbouring Alpine tribes as the campaigns of Augustus extended Roman power into Germania. It is this last phase of expansion of the province that is the subject of this section of the block. This will not be a systematic study of the whole province, but a series of short 'case studies'. The first is the colony at Aosta, where the extension of Roman power led to the creation of a very Roman city and some of the native peoples joined with the Roman settlers. The second is an examination of a monument at Susa, where Roman power and culture can be seen to be encroaching on a native society. The third is a discussion of the effects of the Roman conquest on some of the native tribes around Trento.

For your work in this section you will need to use Goodman, Wells, Lewis and Reinhold and the Illustrations Book.

Exercise

Read (1) Goodman, pages 135–7 'Allies or subjects?' and 'Roman citizenship'; (2) Goodman, pages 221–3 'The Alps'; (3) Wells, page 84 (fourth line) to the top of page 85. These will provide you with essential background information for the areas of the empire you will now be studying.

Discussion

In passage (1) Goodman briefly discusses some possible relationships between Romans and non-Romans and the spread of citizenship. In passage (2) the Roman conquest of the Alpine region is outlined. In passage (3) the Augustan development of the cities of Cisalpine Gaul and the conquest of the Alpine valleys is described. Together they show that the Roman conquest and development of the mountain fringes was a complex process involving military conquest, changes in status and identity and also changes in ways of living. We are now going to look at some of the places mentioned in these extracts in more detail in order to examine some aspects of the Romanization of this area and the establishment of the limits of Roman Italy.

Augusta Pretoria (Aosta)

The conquest of the tribe of the Salassi, who lived in the valley of the Dora Baltea and controlled the Great St Bernard Pass over the Alps, was described by Strabo (*Geography* 4.6.7) (quoted by Goodman, p.222) and Cassius Dio (*Roman History* 53.25). The tribe was conquered in 25 BC and Augustus founded a city in their territory. The city was called Colonia Augusta Pretoria (its modern name of Aosta derives from this). The extract by Strabo says that of the 36,000 tribe members captured, 8,000 soldiers were sold into slavery. We cannot be sure what became of the others, but the 3,000 veterans of the Praetorian Guard (the emperor's bodyguard) who were to populate the city were not the only inhabitants of the new town. An inscription from Aosta dating from 23–22 BC was dedicated in honour of Augustus by some of the Salassi, who are described as being inhabitants of the colony (*colonia*) from the beginning. So it seems that the people of the city were a mixture of retired Italian soldiers who were Roman citizens (ex-Praetorian Guards) and some of the Alpine tribe. It appears that the tribe was first militarily suppressed and subsequently integrated into the Roman city.

We know about the events leading up to the founding of Augusta Pretoria but Aosta also happens to be extremely well-preserved, and so we can look at some of the physical remains of the Roman city built in the lands of the conquered Salassi. In the following exercise you will be asked to identify features of the city on a plan and then these features will be discussed so that you become familiar with the city.

Exercise

Look at the plan of the Roman remains of Aosta (Plate 2.2).

Locate the enclosing walls of the city which are labelled on the plan. They are marked with a black line and form a rectangular shape enclosing all the other features on the plan. Supporting buttresses are marked as small dots on the interior face of the walls. The walls enclose a rectangle of 41.5 hectares (approximately 100 acres). Augusta Pretoria was a fortified city, suited to ex-Praetorian Guards, and its 10-metre-high walls were defended by twelve square towers at regular intervals (Plate 2.3).

On each straight stretch of the walls you can count four towers. Some of the towers have not survived and these are marked with dotted lines where their plan has been reconstructed (as are all the features which have not survived but may be reconstructed).

Altogether the city has four gates (Plate 2.4), marked as gaps in the walls on the plan. The eastern gate bars the road to Italy via Turin to Rome; the western gate bars the road to Gaul crossing the Little St Bernard Pass; the northern gate bars the road to Helvetica (Switzerland) and Germania. The location of the city, blocking the bottom of a narrow valley which leads to the Alpine passes to Gaul and Germany, is clearly highly strategic, and the military and logistical reasons for placing a city at that point are compelling. Thus the city protected the route into Italy from the north and west from both marauding barbarian tribes and potential imperial rivals in times of civil war (see Figure 2.1).

Figure 2.1 *View down the Dora Baltea valley showing the strategic location of Aosta. (Photo: Phil Perkins)*

The main streets of the city, leading from gate to gate, do not meet in the centre of the city and this feature is typical of military camps of the period as well as other cities. So the settlement has some military features to suit its location and its ex-soldier Roman citizens. The chessboard grid of its streets, which substantially survives in the plan of the modern town, is largely reconstructed on Plate 2.2: the actual remains of the roads with drains beneath and street frontages have only been located in a few places. If the street plan is projected on to the entire area within the walls and made to match up with the towers of the walls, Roman Aosta would have had sixty-four equal-sized rectangular city blocks. However, the remains of the city buildings do not perfectly conform to this ideal plan.

Locate the oval amphitheatre on the plan. How many 'ideal' city blocks does it occupy? The amphitheatre in the north-east corner of the city occupies two ideal blocks. Locate the theatre on the plan. The theatre occupies the block to the south of the amphitheatre, and the curved plan of the seating is apparent on the plan. Does it perfectly fit into the ideal grid plan of the city? The theatre fills one block and its straight wall forms a street frontage; however, the north and east walls of the building are not aligned with the ideal street grid.

To the north-east of the point where the two principal streets cross, the ideal plan of city blocks is interrupted and some large buildings occupy what would be eight of them. In the northern part is a large structure enclosing three sides of a rectangle, leaving the southern side open. This building is a cryptoporticus, a subterranean structure with a double-barrel vault supported on piers along its axis (Plate 2.5). Within the enclosed area is a rectangular structure. This is the podium of a temple (Plate 2.6). This temple is not placed centrally in the cryptoporticus and it may have been one of a pair of temples, the other of which has not survived. To the south of this an area of paving has been excavated and further south are more paving and a portico with rooms behind aligned with the street grid and the cryptoporticus. These are the remains of the paving of the forum – an open square or piazza – and a surrounding portico. The cryptoporticus and the temple form the capitol on the northern side of this forum (Plate 2.7). Together the forum and capitol form the centre of the city.

Other buildings on the plan are shops, houses, possibly a market building, a temple and a bath complex. Later on in the block you will be doing some more exercises reading plans of Roman cities which will develop your plan-reading skills further.

The public buildings in Aosta are typical of Roman cities in other parts of Italy: a temple within a portico, a colonnaded forum, a theatre and an amphitheatre, and a bath building. Later in the block you will meet such buildings again in Pompeii and Ostia.

The *colonia* or colony has a long tradition in the Roman world. The earliest known colonies date back to the fourth century BC, for example at Ostia, where the wall of a central rectangular core of the early city is still preserved.

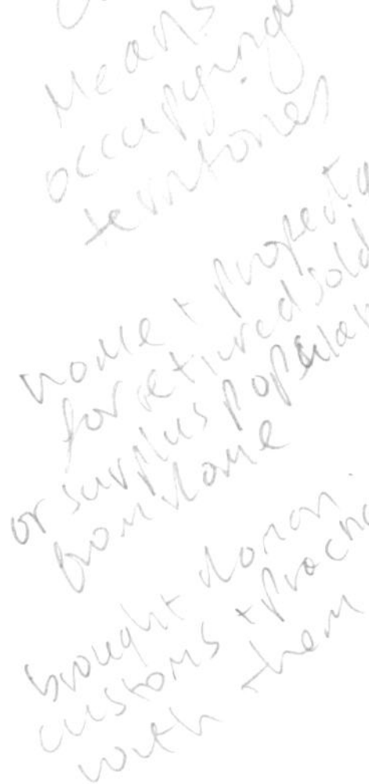

Colonies were used as a means of occupying territories which had been conquered by Roman armies, so for example Cosa was built in the territory of the conquered Etruscans of the city of Vulci just as Aosta was built in the territory of the Salassi some 250 years later. The use of the colonies to provide a home and property for retired soldiers or surplus population from the city of Rome guaranteed the loyalty of the new city, as well as ensuring that the inhabitants would be able to defend themselves against any resentful newly conquered local tribes. Furthermore, the settlers were familiar with Roman ways of life and brought Roman customs and practices with them. The colonies also contributed to creating Italian identity by enrolling non-Romans as colonists and giving them partial rights of citizenship (in so-called Latin colonies) and by scattering Roman citizens up and down the peninsula.

Colonies are common throughout Italy and in Gallia Cisalpina and by the time of Augustus a new wave of colonization was taking place in the area, driven by two factors: firstly the large number of demobilized veterans retiring after the many years of civil war who were rewarded with grants of land, and secondly the Roman conquest of the Alpine region and Germania to the north, which had added new territory to the empire. Aosta fits into this scenario since it was built in newly conquered territory and protected the route northwards to Germania. Several of the colonies in Gallia Cisalpina are similar to Aosta, for example Colonia Iulia Augusta Taurinorum (modern Turin), founded in 28 BC, where the street grid survives in the modern city plan, and Novum Comum (modern Como), where the street plan is also well preserved. These and other colonies were not simply isolated cities: their surrounding territory was also divided up into blocks of land (*centuriae*) and each colonist was assigned a block to farm. In some areas traces of this division of land (centuriation) has survived and can be detected on aerial photographs and maps, for example near the town of Cesena (the modern name is the same) in eastern Gallia Cisalpina (Plate 2.8).

So the foundation of regular Roman-style cities and the standardized division and redistribution of land to incoming Roman settlers formed one part of the process of Romanization in Gallia Cisalpina as it became incorporated into Italia.

Augustus and Cottius at Susa

If we return briefly to Aosta, one major monument we have not yet considered is a large triumphal arch outside the city walls which crosses the road to Rome. It is similar in form and purpose to the later arch of Titus, which you have studied in the video sequence 'Emperor and empire' in Block One. The arch at Aosta was erected to commemorate the victory of Augustus over the Salassi. It formed a material and symbolic reminder of the Roman conquest. The inscription on the arch doesn't survive, but further west another arch at modern Susa is better preserved.

Susa, like Aosta, occupies a strategic location at the foot of the Mont Cénis pass across the Alps to Gaul. The arch commemorates Augustus, and was constructed in 9–8 BC (Plate 2.9a). At the top is an inscription, originally in bronze letters. The text states that the arch was dedicated to Augustus by Marcus Julius Cottius, that is, king Cottius I, son of king Donnus, and he is given the title of Prefect (governor) of fourteen different tribes. The conspicuous inscription first prominently names Augustus, along with his formal political, military and religious titles, on the first line. On the second line Cottius is named, in smaller characters, and his pedigree is given. He is 'son of *king* Donnus' whereas Augustus is described as 'son of a *god*', surely denoting his superiority. Cottius is then given his formal title as Prefect of the peoples who comprise the new province of Alpes Cottiae, who are then listed.

On the arch below the inscription is a frieze. Look carefully at the frieze sculptures from the south side of the arch (Plate 2.9a). It is difficult to see on the photograph, but from the left the frieze shows a naked figure standing in front of a horse. It is not obvious who this might be but naked figures are usually divinities in Roman art. This is followed by four foot soldiers and then two armed horsemen walking and riding towards the right. On Plate 2.9b the first figures to appear on the left are four standing figures, two with horns and two carrying axes; these last are lictors, the bodyguard of a consul or senior magistrate. After this and also walking towards the right are a pig led by a figure, another figure, a bull led by a figure, two more figures, then another wearing a toga, with a draped head and therefore representing a priest. This figure is dressed to perform a sacrifice at the garlanded altar which lies at the centre of the frieze. The other half of the frieze is almost a mirror image of the left and all the figures are walking left towards the altar. A figure on the right of the altar is an assistant at the ceremony, and next to him is another figure dressed in a toga: this is Cottius dressed as Prefect and accompanied by three lictors. Beside these is another bull with a figure, a sheep with two figures, two horsemen, five foot soldiers and a second naked figure with a horse. Together with the similar figure on the far left we have Castor and Pollux, the *Dioscuri*, particular protectors of the city of Rome.

The scene represents a sacrifice – the *suovetaurilia*, the sacrifice of a pig, a sheep and a bull, one of the most solemn Roman sacrifices, but here two bulls are represented. The various figures closest to the altar are the assistants to the priest. The figure on the right side of the altar, behind an attendant, is presumably Cottius again in the act of swearing allegiance to Augustus, who is acting as the priest to the left of the altar.

Overall, what we have here is a traditional style of Roman commemorative arch set up by a client king and representing his act of allegiance to Rome. Cottius is appropriating a Roman form of commemoration to do honour to Augustus. The act of swearing the allegiance is represented in the frieze and so Cottius, a native king, is participating in a very solemn Roman ceremony as his identity and status are transformed from Celtic king into Roman governor in the presence of Augustus, Castor and Pollux. The form of the relief is a typical Roman way of depicting historical events in pictures, and this all happens beneath a large Latin inscription, not the language of the Celtic Gauls.

Although the actions represented on the frieze are clearly Roman, the style of representation is not classically Roman. If we compare the priestly figure of Augustus with the statue of Augustus as *pontifex maximus* which you have already studied in Block One, section 1.2 (Plate 1.4), the difference is striking. The arch relief is much less precisely executed, and none of the idealizing and perfect aspects of the statue are apparent. The

Augustus figure does not resemble the canonical Augustus and there is little to differentiate his features from any of those of the other figures. The proportions of the figure are not anatomically accurate. Why might this be? Perhaps the sculptor was not very skilled, or perhaps the image of Augustus was not familiar to the artist. Clearly, we are not dealing with the refined art of the city of Rome. It is possible that the sculptor was a Gaul working in a Gaulish rather than a Roman tradition.

The arch straddles the road from Gaul towards Italy and would be the first thing that travellers would see as they decended from the Alpine pass and approached the city of Susa. The representation of Cottius and Augustus on the arch is associating the two for all to see and combining Gaulish with Roman power. So here we have an illustration of Roman culture being taken up by a Gaulish king, but there is a different relation of power from that commemorated on the triumphal arch at Aosta: in the Val d'Aosta the Salassi were conquered and political control passed to the Roman colonists, whereas at Susa the pre-existing power structure survived and the king, after initially resisting, became an ally of Augustus and ruled his lands peacefully. We can see this in the decoration of the Susa arch, for usually Roman arches are extensively decorated with trophies from military victories and images of vanquished foes: here there are none and the arch commemorates a treaty rather than a triumphal victory. The tribes remained an ally of Rome until the death of king Cottius II in AD 63, when the kingdom became a Roman province.

Figure 2.2 *Early second-century AD silver bust of Jupiter depicted as a Gaul, from Aosta. Museo Archeologico, Aosta. (Photo: Phil Perkins)*

Problems of citizenship

A bronze inscription from AD 46 (reproduced on pages 51–2 of Lewis and Reinhold) concerns the status of some people living alongside the Roman citizens of the Roman municipality of Tridentum (modern Trento). This area lies on the edge of Gallia Cisalpina but it is not clear when or how the Tridentines received citizenship. Citizenship gave legal rights and status and was commonly used as a tool to integrate conquered peoples with those who were already Roman citizens. The inscription shows us that there were still some loose ends in the time of Claudius (whom you have met in Block One) and some people had missed out on or been excluded from the grant of citizenship. You will be studying the nature of citizenship in more detail later in the block when you read Essay Five on 'Status and identity in the Roman world'.

The inscription is an edict (*edictum*). An edict was a public publication by a senior magistrate, provincial governor or *pontifex* which announced either new laws or modifications of existing laws. In the republican period edicts had to be tested in the courts before they were accepted as laws, but in the imperial period they became the standard means by which an emperor created or changed laws, technically using his office as a magistrate (usually consul).

The first part of the inscription dates the edict and tells which emperor issued it. The next concerns the people of Como and the Bergaleians, but we are not going to be concerned with that part in detail. It is the final part which interests us because it reveals how it is possible for there to be a grey area between being a Roman citizen and a non-citizen.

Exercise

Read the inscription in Lewis and Reinhold, pages 50–2 (*CIL*, vol. V, no. 5,050) now, and as you read each paragraph pause and write a brief summary of what it says.

Now write brief answers to the following questions.

1 How is the edict given power and authority in the first two paragraphs?

2 Which identities are referred to in the fifth paragraph?

Discussion

1 The first two paragraphs demonstrate the power of the emperor: his full name, titles and powers are given, the powers being religious or honorific (*pontifex maximus*, father of his country), legal and constitutional (tribunician power and consul) and

military (*imperator*). The edict receives its power and authority by virtue of the fact that it was issued by the emperor, using his constitutional powers. In the third paragraph the power of the emperor to delegate the authority to solve local disputes is also clearly demonstrated. Furthermore, Claudius is differentiating his careful and attentive government from the negligence of Tiberius and Gaius' dangerous unpredictability.

2 Identity is also central to the content of the inscription. Apart from different groups of people being identified either as Tridentines – the people of a city – or as Anaunians, Tulliassians and Sindunians – the people of a tribe – the whole question of the last two paragraphs is whether the tribespeople are to have the identity of Roman citizens – another form of identity. The problem the edict resolves arose because the Tridentines were Roman citizens and the other tribes officially were not, even though they lived alongside the Tridentines. This confusion of identities had led to a series of paradoxes because the élite Praetorian Guard was supposed to be composed of Italians at this time and only Roman citizens could take part in legal cases at Rome. There was also the fact that the identities and status of the other tribes were established by long usage and they could not practically be separated from the Tridentines without disrupting the city. Therefore Claudius resolves the problem by giving all of the people legitimate identity and status as Roman citizens, and also allowing them to keep Roman-style names. The episode recalls the letter of Claudius to the Alexandrians you studied in Block One (section 3.2), in which Claudius is also recorded as communicating with a local community and trying to solve its problems.

Culture is not directly addressed in the inscription, but we are told that some of the Anaunians, the Tulliassians and the Sindunians were participating in the culture of the city of Rome by joining an élite military unit, participating in the Roman legal system and generally acting as Romans.

So now that we have studied this case in detail, do you think the Anaunians, the Tulliassians and the Sindunians were Romans before the edict was issued? It is easy enough to answer this question with a simple 'No', because otherwise Claudius would not have needed to clarify their status and grant them citizenship. However, they had become mixed with the Roman citizens of Tridentum and participated in Roman affairs, and so in practice they were indistinguishable from Roman citizens. Wells, in his brief mention of this edict (bottom of p.84 to top of p.85), implies that the tribes had manipulated affairs by using the words 'were allowed to usurp citizenship' to describe their actions, but this is not what the inscription says. However, the inscription could also be read as showing that Claudius was being pragmatic in solving the problem, and even magnanimous in generously granting these people rights which they did not really have a claim to. The difference between these points of view is that Wells presents citizenship as something that the tribes were clamouring to receive so as to become more Roman, whereas we are suggesting that it was something that emperors were keen to bestow in order to make the tribes more Roman. The two points of view are not necessarily contradictory, but demonstrate different ways of looking at the same issue. Another possible interpretative angle is that the edict was not issued to benefit the tribespeople but rather to advantage the Praetorian Guard and their officer cadre who had put Claudius in power (see Goodman, p.54), some of whom directly benefited from him sorting out this knotty problem. However, these niceties of the politics of Claudius' principate may have been missed by many Tridentine readers, even if the unnamed Praetorian commanders concerned might have been aware that Claudius was paying his debts.

The limits of Italy

In 7–6 BC, when Augustus had finally subdued all the tribes of the Alps, he set up a massive monument, 50 metres tall, at La Turbie above Monaco and overlooking the road built in 13 BC to link Italy with Gaul (Plate 2.10). The monument, the Tropaeum Alpium (trophy of the Alps), celebrates the conquest of the peoples of the Alps. The inscription reads:

> To the Emperor Caesar, son of the late lamented Augustus [Julius Caesar], Supreme Pontiff, in his fourteenth year of office as commander in chief and his seventeenth year of tribunician power – erected by the Senate and People of Rome, to commemorate that under his leadership and auspices all the Alpine peoples stretching from the Adriatic Sea to the Mediterranean were brought under the dominion of the Roman people. Alpine peoples conquered – the Triumpilini, Camunni ... Salassi ...

Altogether forty-seven peoples are listed. They do not include the subjects of Cottius because they were already allies.

The Tropaeum Alpium is a monument to the political and military power of the Roman people and Augustus. It also symbolizes the dominance of Roman culture over the uncivilized Alpine tribes by placing a massive Roman-style monument on the summit of the Alps where the mountains meet the Mediterranean sea. The monument and the arches at Susa and Aosta, each clearly bearing the name of Augustus, also combine to mark the limits of Italy and the beginnings of the provinces of Gaul.

In 6 BC Augustus reorganized the administration of Italy into eleven regions (*regiones*) and reset its boundaries. The functions and purpose of these *regiones* are not known, but may have been related to general administration or census operations. By this time most of Cisalpine Gaul (apart from some Alpine areas) was thoroughly developed and most of its people were Roman citizens. Augustus made Cisalpine Gaul a part of Italy, with the Alps as its natural frontier. At the same time Roman military power was extending the boundaries of the empire beyond the Alps into Germania, Raetia and Noricum.

So now Cisalpine Gaul had become four of the regions of Italy: Liguria, Gallia Transpadana, Gallia Cispadana and Venetia. In the next part of this block we will move on to look at other regions: in Campania, around modern Naples, we will study Pompeii and in Latium we will investigate Ostia.

Part Two: Rome, Pompeii and Ostia

BY VALERIE HOPE AND PHIL PERKINS

In this part of Block Two you will study two Italian towns – Pompeii and Ostia. Both sites are special because their high levels of preservation provide unique insights into their appearance and organization and life within the towns. Pompeii and Ostia represent two distinct areas of Italy and the towns differed in origins and influences. Both were united, however, by the dominance of Rome. You will consider the impact of Rome on both Pompeii and Ostia and explore some of the similarities and differences between Roman towns.

2.1 Locating Pompeii and Ostia

This section aims to provide you with some background information and preparatory skills before the rest of your work on Pompeii and Ostia. The history, both ancient and modern, of the two sites will be summarized and the plans of Pompeii and Ostia introduced. You will need to have Goodman, Wells and the Illustrations Book to hand, and will also be listening to audio cassette 1.

To ensure that you are familiar with the locations of Pompeii and Ostia, look at the map of Italy on page 192 of Goodman, Plate 2.11 in the Illustrations Book, Map 2(b) in Wells and the A2 site plans.

Ostia is to be found on the coast a short distance from the city of Rome. Plate 2.11 shows the road and river connections between Rome and Ostia.

Pompeii is to be found further along the same coast on the Bay of Naples. Map 2(b) in Wells provides a detailed plan of the Bay of Naples highlighting towns of historical significance, including Pompeii and Herculaneum which were destroyed by the volcano Vesuvius, the location of which is also indicated.

Now turn to the A2 site plans of Pompeii and Ostia. These represent the excavated remains of the two cities. At first sight these plans may seem complex and their usefulness in reconstructing the ancient cities limited. You will recall, however, that earlier in this block you looked at a plan of Aosta and used this to identify and analyse some important features of the Roman town. Plans are a useful way of both summarizing and representing data and it is important that you become familiar with the conventions used in their creation and can relate what is represented on the plan to what exists on the ground.

You should now listen to audio cassette 1, band 2, 'Plan reading I', which introduces you to the subject by studying some plans of buildings found in Rome, Pompeii and Ostia.

To work through this band you will need Plans A–D and Illustrations 1–8 (Plates 2.12–2.23 in the Illustrations Book):

Plan A (Plate 2.12): temple of Portunus in the Forum Boarium, Rome

Plan B (Plate 2.16): theatre, Ostia

Plan C (Plate 2.18): shop-house, Pompeii

Plan D (Plate 2.20): House of the Lovers, Pompeii

Illustration 1 (Plate 2.13): north façade of temple of Portunus

Illustration 2 (Plate 2.14): east façade of temple of Portunus

Illustration 3 (Plate 2.15): temple of Portunus

Illustration 4 (Plate 2.17): theatre at Ostia before reconstruction

Illustration 5 (Plate 2.19): shop-house, Pompeii

Illustration 6 (Plate 2.21): House of the Lovers

Illustration 7 (Plate 2.22): House of the Lovers

Illustration 8 (Plate 2.23): House of the Lovers

During this band you are asked to work through the following questions.

Exercise 1 (Plan A)

How would someone standing due south of the temple reach the interior of the *cella*?

Is there any way to estimate the height of the podium?

How many columns did the temple have, and how far apart are they?

Exercise 2 (Plan B)

Where would the performers have stood?

How many sets of stairs can you see in the theatre?

Can you work out what the dotted lines indicate?

Exercise 3 (Plan C)

How many entrances does the shop-house have from the street, and how large are they?

How many rooms are there in total?

Can you see any windows?

Exercise 4 (Plan D)

Which rooms would the occupants of the house have passed through to get from the street to room 10? Would they have had a choice of routes?

How light do you think the different rooms would have been, and what do you think would have been their main source of daylight?

Looking at the organization of interior space and the numbers of rooms opening off different areas, which do you think would have been the busiest parts of the house?

Exercise 5 (Plan D and Illustrations 6, 7 and 8)

Using the plan, can you work out where each photograph was taken from?

What are your reasons for the identification of each location?

Pompeii – history, destruction and preservation

Pompeii was situated on the Bay of Naples in the region of Italy known as Campania (see Wells, Map 2(b)). There was some sort of settlement on the site as early as the seventh century BC. As the town developed it came under diverse influences – Greek, Etruscan, Samnite and native Oscan. Pompeii was connected to the sea by a port on the River Sarno and to neighbouring settlements by a good road network. By the second century BC it had developed into a town of some size and importance and had fallen under the influence of Rome. When the Social War was declared (91 BC) Pompeii was among the first to revolt against Rome. Following the Roman victory it was settled by Roman colonists drawn from military veterans. This settlement would have involved the confiscation of at least some land from the native Pompeians and its redistribution to the colonists. A new constitution and municipal organization were probably also introduced. There may have been some initial tensions between the native Pompeians and the colonists, but by the Augustan period the town appears to have been united. Pompeii continued to prosper, although it did not play a leading role in imperial history. No senators are recorded as originating from Pompeii, nor any leading equestrian officials. Pompeii only graced the pages of history for an infamous riot at the amphitheatre in AD 59 (Tacitus, *Annals* 14.17). The first warning of the disaster to come was a severe earthquake in AD 62 which caused extensive damage to the town (Seneca, *On Natural Philosophy* 6) (see Figure 2.4 in the next section). The degree to which Pompeii had recovered from this before the Vesuvian eruption is unclear.

On 24 and 25 August, AD 79 the eruption of Vesuvius destroyed the town of Pompeii. The Younger Pliny, whose uncle the Elder Pliny was killed while attempting to rescue evacuees, provides a graphic account of the horrors of that day.

> They debated whether to stay indoors or to take their chance in the open, for the buildings were now shaking with violent shocks, and seemed to be swaying to and fro as if they were torn from their foundations. Outside on the other hand, there was the danger of falling pumice-stones, even though these were light and porous; however after comparing the risks they chose the latter. In my Uncle's case one reason outweighed the other, but for the others it was a choice of fears.
>
> (Pliny the Younger, *Letters* 6.16; trans. Radice, 1963, p.163)

The devastating eruption of Vesuvius marked the end of Pompeii, although it is worth noting that the complete disappearance of the town was a process that took days and weeks rather than hours. At least some of the population were successfully evacuated, probably taking many of their belongings with them. After the eruption Pompeii was buried by nearly four metres of pumice and fine ash but in some places the upper parts of walls may have still been visible (Richardson, 1988, p.25). Salvage operations were organized which ranged from the systematic recovery of expensive building materials to people burrowing to discover lost valuables. It may have been some time before the survivors ceased to live near the ruins.

The town was concealed, preserved and forgotten. The exact location of Pompeii remained unknown until the eighteenth century. During the nineteenth century much of the site was uncovered, a process fuelled by the antiquarian interests of the Neapolitan royalty and the desire to find important buildings, precious objects and beautiful paintings. From the mid nineteenth century excavations became more systematic in the search to gain a better overall view of the site. But the speed of excavations often led to poor documentation, publication and preservation (Etienne, 1992, pp.16–38) (see Figure 2.3). Recent decades have seen a greater emphasis on the consolidation and conservation of the excavated remains. New excavations have been limited and resources have been focused on recording what has already been uncovered and protecting it from further decay.

The extent of the remains of Pompeii has captured the popular imagination as no other archaeological site and the town has become a lucrative tourist attraction. In considering Pompeii you need to keep in mind not only its past but also its present. What was and was not preserved by the eruption? Why and how was the town excavated? How are the remains conserved and presented? As an example, consider how the objects found within the buildings have been treated: precious items

Figure 2.3 *Nineteenth-century excavations at Pompeii. (Source: Etienne, 1992, p.31)*

made of gold or silver may have been more readily rescued in antiquity than those judged less valuable; similar judgements of worth may have been made by early excavators in what was retrieved; and once excavated, objects have to be conserved and stored, generally removed from their original environment. Remember the image of a Pompeian wall considered in the Introduction to the Course (Figure 0.1). The central painted panel has been cut away and thus isolated from its original context. Moves like this are sometimes inevitable but can limit subsequent understanding of both spaces and objects.

Ostia – history, destruction and preservation

A settlement developed at Ostia during the fourth century BC. It remains uncertain whether Ostia was founded as a Roman colony, but the proximity of the site to Rome and its location at the mouth of the Tiber (Goodman, Figure 5, p.192) make it difficult to separate the history and development of Ostia from that of the capital city. This is not to say, however, that Ostia was merely a suburb of Rome. It remained a separate and in many ways unique settlement. Ostia's coastal location was good defensively and during the conflicts with Carthage it may have acted as a naval base. It was Ostia's role as a commercial harbour and port that earned it its reputation. From the second century BC Rome was becoming dependent on imported grain and other foreign goods, and it was on this basis that Ostia was a substantial and successful town by the early empire. Ostia was not the only harbour in Italy with access to Rome, however, and the Ostian harbour easily became overcrowded, while the river mouth was unsuitable for large vessels. Under Claudius (AD 41–54) work began on a new harbour two miles to the north of the Tiber which was connected to the river by a new canal. An additional harbour was added by the emperor Trajan (Plate 2.11). The new harbours initially brought increased prosperity to Ostia, reflected in the extensive rebuilding of the urban fabric of the town during the second century AD. But the new harbours were not actually in Ostia and there was, with time, a gradual shift of focus from Ostia to the harbourside settlements. In the fourth and fifth centuries coastal Ostia was particularly vulnerable to the invasions that affected Italy. It was probably not until the ninth century, however, that Ostia was abandoned. Flooding in subsequent centuries caused the course of the Tiber to change and the area became malarial.

The site of ancient Ostia, unlike that of Pompeii, was not forgotten and across the centuries it was heavily looted. Successive invasions and attacks by Goths, Vandals and Saracens robbed Ostia of many treasures, and the destruction and looting continued into the twentieth century. Building materials were salvaged for use in Rome and elsewhere; marble was turned into lime; and statues and inscriptions were removed to private collections. What was left in place was subject to erosion and decay. Sporadic excavations began in the nineteenth century and at the beginning of the twentieth century a new policy was formulated to study the town systematically. In 1938, however, the decision was made to clear the greater part of the site in preparation for the 1942 International Exhibition to be held in Rome. The rapid excavation turned Ostia into an exhibit and in the process valuable evidence was lost (Meiggs, 1973, p.5). The site often presents the ruins as a pleasing spectacle and not necessarily as the excavators unearthed them (see Plate 2.17): walls, for example, have been restored and trees and shrubs dot the site.

Frozen in time?

Pompeii and Ostia are unusual because of the extent and nature of their preservation. At both sites it is possible to stand in the street, visit the baths or look at a house in a Roman townscape in a way that is rarely possible elsewhere in what was the Roman empire. Nevertheless, the differences between Pompeii and Ostia in terms of background, cultural influences and historical development should not be forgotten. This is most apparent in the buildings and structures, since the physical remains of Ostia mainly date to the second century AD whereas Pompeii ceased in the first century AD. Neither site, however, is frozen in time. Ostia's decline was slow and lingering and at Pompeii there was a process of abandonment even if this was more rapid. In addition, the history of the excavation of each site and the methods and underlying motivation for those excavations need to be remembered. Both Pompeii and Ostia have been made into tourist attractions, forcing the available evidence to be presented in a suitable fashion.

2.2 Fora and public buildings

One method of exploring the extent to which Rome influenced towns and settlements is to consider similarities and differences between buildings and urban layouts. To what degree did the towns of Ostia and Pompeii share common features with Rome? And what does this suggest about power relations and the relative culture and identity of each site? In the work on Aosta in Part One of this block you considered some of the elements found in Roman colonies and settlements. In this section you will address this issue further by special reference to the fora (singular: forum) and other public spaces of the towns of Ostia and Pompeii. To what extent did the fora of Ostia and Pompeii resemble those of Rome? And what does this suggest about how Rome and Italian towns interacted in terms of culture and power?

In the course of your work in this section you will acquire more skills in reading plans by means of an audio cassette exercise. Then you will watch a video sequence that explores the fora of Rome, Ostia and Pompeii. You will also need the Illustrations Book and Supplementary Texts to hand.

Now listen to audio cassette 2, band 1, 'Plan reading II'.

To work through this band you will need Plans E–G as well as Plans A–D, which you worked through in the previous plan reading exercises:

Plan E (Plate 2.24): part of Regions I and VIII, Pompeii

Plan F: A2 site plan of Pompeii

Plan G (Plate 2.25): schematic representation of public buildings in Regions I and VIII, Pompeii

During this band you are asked to work through the following questions.

Exercise 1 (Plan E with Plans A–D)

How would you go from the Stabian Gate to building VIII.5.35?

Can you find one example of each of the types of building which are familiar from the first plan reading exercise? (You'll need to look for a temple, a theatre, a shop-house and an atrium house.)

What feature or features are you using to identify each of your examples? (You may want to refer back to Plans A–D, which show the buildings you studied earlier.)

Exercise 2 (Plans D and E)

What similarities and differences do you see between the two plans?

If you were studying the House of the Lovers, what would be the advantages and the disadvantages of using each plan?

Exercise 3 (Plans E and G)

What do the differences between the two plans tell you about the main areas of interest to the draughtsperson of Plan G?

Is there any information which you can get from Plan G which is not given by Plan E?

Roman fora

The plan reading exercises have introduced you to certain buildings and structures found at Rome, Ostia and Pompeii such as theatres, temples and houses. One element that these three settlements also have in common is a forum. The forum was an open space which functioned as a type of town square. Its roles were multiple: it was an informal meeting place, a centre for political assemblies, a location for religious ceremonial, a market area and a focus for entertainment. The open space of the forum was generally surrounded by buildings which reflected its multiple functions – meeting rooms for the town council, hallways for legal proceedings, shops and markets for trade and covered areas for people to stroll in and chat with friends and business associates. In short, the forum was at the heart of the Roman town and in many ways was a feature which marked a town as Roman.

Useful insights into the role and organization of the forum are found in a text dating to the Augustan era. Vitruvius composed a handbook on architecture which he dedicated to the emperor Augustus. Included in this document was a discussion of the design of the forum. Vitruvius' work was aimed at praising and pleasing the emperor and often idealized urban planning and structures. It would be unrealistic to expect to find a forum which looked and functioned exactly like that described by Vitruvius. Nevertheless, the work is still valuable for its overall comments on forum design.

Exercise

You should now read extract 2.1 in the Supplementary Texts.

Make notes on the following:

1 What are the main features of the forum itself and what buildings should surround it?

2 What types of activities take place in the forum?

Discussion

1 Vitruvius begins by noting that the Greek equivalent of the forum (the agora) was square in shape. In contrast the Roman forum was rectangular. Vitruvius notes the ideal proportions for the forum, although its exact dimensions would need to be varied according to the size of the associated population. The space was surrounded by colonnades or porticoes which provided a vantage point for watching gladiatorial contests and shelter for shops and bankers. Vitruvius notes that basilicas ought to adjoin the forum and then describes in detail their relative proportions and design. The other buildings that Vitruvius states should be adjacent to the forum are the treasury, prison and senate house.

2 Vitruvius describes the forum as a public space and notes that it is a venue for both public and private business. He then pays particular attention to the traditional role of the forum as a venue for gladiatorial contests and how this affected the organization of the space. The reference to shops and bankers around the edge of the forum and businessmen in the basilica suggests the commercial and economic role of the forum. The presence of the senate house (*curia*), treasury and prison emphasize that the forum was the seat of the government and administration of the town.

Vitruvius provides us with an idealized plan of a forum and sums up its functions. The description is not all-inclusive, partly because Vitruvius is interested in only some elements of design and layout and also because some features are described elsewhere in his treatise. Thus you may have noted that Vitruvius makes no mention of the forum as a religious centre. This is because his work includes a separate section on the planning of temples. As you will see, many fora of Italian towns contained elements and features similar to those described by Vitruvius. But often fora developed over a period of time, in a piecemeal fashion with little overall planning. Thus it cannot always have been possible or desirable to employ elements such as Vitruvius' ideal proportions for buildings and spaces. Equally, across time some of the roles and functions of the forum changed. Vitruvius' reference to gladiatorial contests in the forum illustrates this well. You may have been surprised by this association, especially if you have visited one of the many surviving Roman amphitheatres such as the Colosseum in Rome. The forum was the original venue for the mass entertainment of the people; but gradually this function devolved to purpose-built structures. By the time of the early empire most Italian towns probably no longer held such spectacles in the forum.

The remainder of your work in this section will focus on the fora of Rome, Pompeii and Ostia, although some other public spaces and structures will be touched on. As your work progresses keep in mind Vitruvius' comments about the roles and appearance of the forum. You should consider the degree to which there was some sort of blueprint for a forum and the extent to which the fora of Rome were similar to those of Ostia and Pompeii. You should also assess how the power and influence of the emperor and other prominent citizens impacted on the appearance and organization of the fora at all three sites.

You will now need the video sequence 'Fora and public buildings' on video cassette 1. It is divided into three sections, on Rome, Ostia and Pompeii. You should watch each section in turn, referring to the supporting material and undertaking the associated exercises.

Rome

This video section (t.c.46:05–1:00:00) explores the Forum Romanum and three of the Imperial Fora of Rome. It focuses on the surviving remains of these fora, the archaeological study of which illustrates the development of the spaces and buildings, their relative dates and their original appearance. For Rome the remains of the fora are further illuminated by literary accounts, inscriptions, coin images and sculptural reliefs.

The plan of the city of Rome (Plate 1.6) indicates the location of the Forum Romanum and the Imperial Fora.

You should note before watching that this sequence pays considerable attention to the emperor Augustus. You may find it useful to look back to your work in Block One, section 1.3 on Augustus' impact on the city of Rome and the video sequence 'Augustus and the Campus Martius'.

Be prepared to pause the video to make notes or to look at the supporting material. You will need to refer to Plates 2.26 and 2.27.

Exercise

As you watch make notes on the following:

1 What features, buildings and structures were characteristic of the fora of Rome?

2 How were the fora of Rome used to glorify the name of the emperor?

Discussion

1 You probably noted that the fora of Rome consisted of open spaces which were generally rectangular in shape. The fora were edged by columned sheltered porticoes raised above the level of the square. Buildings such as temples and basilicas were also to be found along the sides of the forum, and statues and other honorific monuments such as arches were on display. The Forum Romanum provided the model for the later fora. Its irregularity of shape reflects the organic nature of its development: in origin this was not a space that was designed and formally laid out. The buildings that edged the Forum Romanum were also rather haphazard in their articulation and spacing, although Augustus and his successors did their best to overcome this problem. In contrast, the Imperial Fora were planned and built in relatively short periods of time with the principles of symmetry and order in mind. These fora generally followed a similar format in that they were rectangular in shape, with a temple on the principal axis and regular and symmetrical porticoes along the sides. The Imperial Fora were not, however,

identical. For example, shape and size could be dictated by terrain and existing structures. If you look closely at the plan of the Forum of Augustus on Plate 2.27 you can see that the forum was not an exact rectangle since the rear of the temple of Mars was built at an angle. You may recall from your reading of Essay Three, in the section entitled 'Rome, the showcase of the emperor', that according to Suetonius the Forum of Augustus was narrow because he did not wish to eject people from their property. The shape of the back wall may have been dictated by similar considerations. In short, Augustus failed to buy up all the land that he needed for his project and was thus forced to mask the fact that the forum was not symmetrical.

2 During the republic the Forum Romanum became a focal point for the public displays of the wealthy and politically powerful élite. Buildings and statues, either funded by them or voted as honours to them, filled the forum. Under the emperors this process continued, but it was now increasingly focused on the emperor and members of his family. Augustus' impact on the Forum Romanum is a fine illustration. Under Augustus the forum became almost a trophy monument to the ruling dynasty. This process was taken a stage further by the construction of the so-called Imperial Fora, which were funded and named after individual emperors. These public gifts provided Rome and its inhabitants with the amenities and facilities of a capital city, but their grandeur and splendour also promoted the name of the emperor.

Ostia

The next section of the video explores the forum and some of the associated public buildings in Ostia. Before watching this look at the A2 site plan of Ostia.

Exercise

Without looking at the labels, can you find the forum? What criteria did you employ to identify it?

Discussion

The Ostian forum is to be found slightly to the west of the centre of the plan. You probably identified it because of its rectangular shape and the temple at its northern end. Did you also spot the dots which represent the columns of the porticoes along its long sides and the rectangular columned building on the west side identified as a basilica? Other buildings at the edges of the forum may have also fulfilled public roles, acting, for example, as the senate house, treasury or prison. But unfortunately the poor state of the surviving remains does not always allow us to ascribe specific functions to buildings. One feature which may have initially confused you is that a road runs through the Ostian forum, effectively cutting it in half. The fora of Rome were shut off from traffic but elsewhere the forum could develop at a major intersection of roads.

Exercise

Still looking at the plan, can you identify any other spaces or structures which may have functioned as public meeting places? (A clue: you've already looked at one of these in the first plan reading exercises.)

Discussion

In your initial search for the forum you may have identified several open spaces. One example is found to the east of the forum and this is known as the 'Forum of the Heroic Statue'. This is a modern label and the role of this porticoed space is uncertain. You should note that the term 'forum' is sometimes employed by the producers of modern plans as a blanket term for an open space. To the south of the Forum of the Heroic Statue is a triangular open space leading off from the forum proper. This was part of the complex known as the Forum Baths. The triangular space was a *palaestra* (exercise area) and the irregularly shaped rooms along its one side were a bathing complex. Ostia had several bathing establishments and these acted as places for relaxation and informal meetings. Further east you may have spotted a semi-circular structure with a large open square beyond. You should have recognized this as the theatre from Exercise 1 of the 'Plan reading I' exercises. Now you can see the theatre in relation to the rest of the town. The open square behind the theatre may have been designed as part of the theatre complex but it appears to have fulfilled the role of a meeting place for tradesmen and ship owners whose premises surrounded it, hence its Italian title of *Foro* (or *Piazzale*) *delle Corporazioni*.

You should now watch the video section (t.c.1:00:44–1:06:00). Keep the plan of Ostia open for reference. Once more be prepared to pause the video at key points if you so wish.

The Ostian forum was similar in many respects to the fora of Rome. A temple dominated the rectangular space which was edged by porticoes and a basilica. A comparison between the plan of the Ostian forum with that of the Forum of Augustus makes the similarities apparent (compare the A2 site plan of Ostia with Plate 2.27). The architectural parallels are echoed by functional ones. The Ostian forum, like the fora of Rome, was a business, commercial, religious and administrative centre. Equally, like the fora of Rome it was a focus for the display of power, both of the local élite and of the Roman emperor. Yet the Ostian forum and its other public facilities uniquely reflect the history and development of the town. Note how the forum was updated – the *capitolium* was added and the porticoes may have been improved – during the reign of Hadrian, a time when Ostia was enjoying economic prosperity following the harbour extensions of Trajan (Meiggs, 1973, pp.74–7). Likewise, the adaptation of the square beyond the theatre reflects the importance of trade and commerce to the town and its cosmopolitan nature. Ostia owed its success to Rome and was always overshadowed by its dominant neighbour, but the town still retained a sense of individuality.

Pompeii

The final section focuses on Pompeii. Before watching look at the A2 site plan of Pompeii.

Exercise

Once more, can you identify the forum?

Discussion

The forum is to be found towards the bottom of the plan in the south-west of the city. You probably noted its rectangular shape and familiar structures such as temples, porticoes and a basilica. Several roads lead to the Pompeian forum, but they do not appear to have crossed the space as at Ostia. In fact, at Pompeii stone bollards were used at the entrances to the forum to block access to wheeled traffic, thus making this a pedestrian area.

Exercise

Can you identify any other spaces or structures that may have acted as public meeting places? (Once more, some of these will be familiar to you from the plan reading exercises.)

Discussion

In the lower part of the plan you probably spotted the so-called Triangular Forum. This does not resemble the fora which you have encountered so far. This is a modern label and this space may not have fulfilled any of the functions associated with a forum. Nevertheless, judging from its proximity to both a temple and the theatre complex, this was an area that would often have been filled with crowds of people. You will have recognized the two theatres and the open space to the south of them from your work in the plan reading exercises. Did you also spot the series of concentric ovals in the east of the plan? This represents the Pompeian amphitheatre. Adjacent to it is a large square space which may have functioned as a precinct for the amphitheatre or as a *palaestra*. If you refer back to the site plan of Ostia you will note that there is no amphitheatre marked. It is unclear whether the Ostians held gladiatorial spectacles elsewhere, such as in the forum, or if the site of the amphitheatre remains undiscovered.

Figure 2.4 *Plaster cast of a marble relief showing scenes of the earthquake of* AD *62 (original from the house of L. Caecilius Jucundus). The relief shows the collapse of the capitol at the northern end of the forum, its steps flanked by a pair of equestrian statues. On the left is a monumental arch, of which the core still survives, and on the right is an altar surrounded by vessels and instruments for the sacrifice of a bull. Museo della Civiltà Romana, Rome.*

You should now watch the video section on Pompeii (t.c.1:06:02–1:16:20). Pause the video and take notes where you feel appropriate. You may also find it useful to refer to Plates 2.28, 2.30, 2.38 and 2.49, Figure 2.4 above and extract 2.2 in the Supplementary Texts.

A translation of the inscription in Plate 2.30 is given in the 'Reading inscriptions' exercise in section 2.3 below (p.42), and a translation of the inscription on the building in Plate 2.38 is given in Lewis and Reinhold, page 369.

Exercise

As you watch make notes on the following:

1 Which structures and features can be classed as 'Roman' introductions to Pompeii?

2 Who paid for the public buildings of Pompeii and to whom were they dedicated?

Discussion

1 In terms of its public amenities Pompeii provides an opportunity to explore the interrelationship between Rome and Italy. In contrast to Ostia, which through its geographic proximity and

economic dependence was always dominated by Rome, at Pompeii it is possible to trace the diverse influences that affected the town. Pompeii has what can be considered the standard elements of a Roman settlement. The video section examined the forum, basilica, temples, theatres and amphitheatre. Additional features such as bathing complexes and other temples could also have been considered. But few of these structures can be simply described as Roman. Before the advent of direct Roman authority Pompeii already had a forum, temples, a basilica and a theatre. These were features of many Italian towns which developed in tandem with similar structures and amenities in Rome itself and often reflected contact with the Greek and Hellenistic world as much as with Rome. After the colonization of Pompeii the Roman influence was felt more directly in the town. Some new facilities were introduced; but the old town was not abandoned or completely remodelled in Rome's image. After all, Pompeii had a stone amphitheatre before Rome did! In the imperial period and the final phase of the town it is possible to identify some close parallels between Pompeii and Rome. The arches of the forum and the Eumachia building, for example, imitated, in design and dedication, structures found in the capital city.

2 Inscriptions suggest that the citizens of Pompeii paid for its buildings and amenities. The leading magistrates acted as benefactors, improving their city as the emperor improved Rome. Similarly, like the emperor these leading citizens gained prestige and glory by their generosity. The local civic pride which improved Pompeii also coexisted with a sense of Roman identity. In the imperial period buildings were often linked to the emperor – the Eumachia building celebrated harmony in the imperial family, a temple promoted the cult of the emperor and arches and statues probably further recalled the imperial family. These buildings thus recorded either real or hoped-for connections between the élite of Pompeii on the one hand and Rome and the emperor on the other.

It is difficult to know whether certain emperors encouraged such expressions of allegiance or whether they were spontaneous gestures on the part of towns such as Pompeii. We cannot dismiss the possibility that Pompeii received imperial patronage and funds. Elsewhere in the empire emperors directly funded public buildings and projects. Emperors might be particularly generous following natural disasters. For example, Tiberius promised money and remitted debts for Sardis and other cities in Asia following an earthquake in AD 17 (Tacitus, *Annals*

2.47). It is possible that after the earthquake of AD 62 (see Figure 2.4) Pompeii received emergency aid from Rome, although there is no direct evidence for this (Dobbins, 1994).

Although some structures may have been funded by the emperor, the appearance and organization of Pompeii did not simply imitate that of Rome; instead the development of Pompeii depended on its own history and diverse influences. Rome was one of these influences and from the first century BC a dominant one. But the town did not simply or dramatically become 'Roman'. The forum, for example, illustrates a continuing process of negotiating both Pompeian and Roman identity. The forum of Pompeii was similar to the fora of Rome but not identical to them. The changes that occurred to the forum at Pompeii after the establishment of the colony were gradual and many of these alterations and improvements might have occurred eventually with or without the Roman colonists. Even then the forum was not completely reshaped. In its final guise before the eruption, when the distinctions between Roman settlers and native Pompeians had been blurred by a hundred years, the forum still combined both pre-Roman and Roman elements. So, for example, the temple to Apollo and the basilica existed alongside the temple to the emperor and the Eumachia building. At this time the dominant method by which the structures of the Pompeian forum were aligned with Rome was through the name of the emperor, which was often placed alongside the names of the ruling élite. The power of the Pompeian élite was enhanced by this association with Roman power: 'sponsors and donors had more in mind than simply the effect of their gifts on their fellow citizens; their gaze was fixed on places further afield, especially Rome' (Zanker, 1998, p.77). Thus the forum in Pompeii became closely aligned with those in Rome less because of its history, development or individual structures and more because overall it increasingly echoed the ideology of the imperial family.

Summary – buildings and identity

The public buildings of a town both reflect and construct an identity for the inhabitants of that town (Laurence, 1994, p.20). In ancient Pompeii and Ostia the buildings, on a general level, suggested a Roman identity. Many structures found in the settlements were parallel to those found in the capital city. The forum is a prime example of this: in simple terms the fora of Pompeii and Ostia were similar to the fora of Rome. These structures and buildings were also more than mere monuments to the Roman presence since they were active spaces which suggested that the inhabitants were following Roman customs. Remember how Vitruvius associated specific functions and activities with specific buildings around the forum. The layout of the forum, then, indicated that a community was similar to Rome not just in appearance but also in its political, social, religious and administrative structures. Roman-style rule demanded Roman-style facilities. The ideal was that across the empire people were united by their attendance at the theatre, amphitheatre and baths and by their visits to the forum, the symbol and centre of a Roman-style administration. The buildings could also create and support a Roman-style hierarchy. The theatre, for example, might be dedicated to the emperor, its construction paid for or overseen by the leading magistrates of the town and its interior ordered to reflect the social structure of the settlement. To attend a show was to be reminded of one's membership of and place in both Ostian or Pompeian society and also the Roman world.

The relationship between buildings, people and a Roman lifestyle is an issue to keep in mind as your work on the course progresses. How much can be inferred from architectural evidence about how people actually lived? To what extent is it possible to reconstruct what happened in the spaces and buildings of a town? Was a town Roman because in some respects it looked like Rome? It is particularly difficult to provide definitive answers to these questions in relation to Italy since its history was closely entwined with that of Rome. Often when we speak of Roman buildings, facilities, amenities and administration we could equally describe these things as Italian. If some Italian towns resembled Rome it was as much because Rome was in Italy as because Italy was in the Roman empire. The forum, for example, was part of a common heritage for which there was no simple blueprint. It might be possible to define, as Vitruvius did, the basic features of a forum, but the development and use of these could reflect localized needs and traditions. Remember that when describing the requirements for his ideal forum Vitruvius is speaking of Italian towns, not just of Rome.

An illustration of localized development is the way in which the forum was a focus not just for expressions of allegiance to Rome and the emperor but also for local civic pride. Once some of the traditional functions of the forum were devolved to new spaces, such as theatres, amphitheatres and market complexes, and especially if the space became pedestrianized, the forum could gain in dignity and become a focus for the display of power. Rome and the emperor could be at the heart of this power display but the relationship was often mediated by the local élite to define and enhance their own power and authority. Rome might be dominant but Roman symbols could be very significant as a method of constructing and negotiating local power and identity.

The desire or the need to appear 'Roman' may, then, have been of greater significance to some than to others. The view gained through civic architecture of the interaction between Rome on the one hand, and towns such as Pompeii and Ostia on the other, is an élite and a public one. Fora, theatres and amphitheatres may have been intended for the use of all but they often reinforced a status hierarchy which benefited the public reputations of the minority. Private sentiments towards Rome and how loyalty, power and identity should or should not be expressed and constructed may have differed greatly. In the next section you will explore some issues concerning the individual identity of the inhabitants of Pompeii and Ostia and how they defined themselves.

2.3 The inhabitants

The remains of the buildings of Pompeii and Ostia preserve at least some aspects of the appearance and organization of the two towns, but this means little without people to occupy the spaces. Who lived in the buildings, visited the forum and wandered through the streets? In many ways it is difficult to get close to people. The plaster casts of the corpses of those killed by the eruption of Vesuvius sometimes provide us with glimpses of the last anguished moments of individuals (see Figure 2.5) but in general it is not possible to reconstruct personal and individual stories. Even speaking of the population in general terms can present problems. This is well illustrated by attempts to estimate the population of Pompeii (Wallace-Hadrill, 1994, pp.95–103), which have ranged from 2,000 to 20,000 people! It may not be possible to quantify impressions, but we can at least acknowledge that the population was not homogeneous. Differences in the inhabitants have already been touched on in discussions of who funded buildings in Pompeii and Ostia and seating arrangements in the theatre and amphitheatre. The evidence restricts what can be said, but it is possible to speak in general terms about groups of people and the interaction between them: élite and non-élite, slave and free, male and female and so forth.

To work through this section you will need *Experiencing Rome*, Lewis and Reinhold and the Supplementary Texts. You will also listen to more of audio cassette 2.

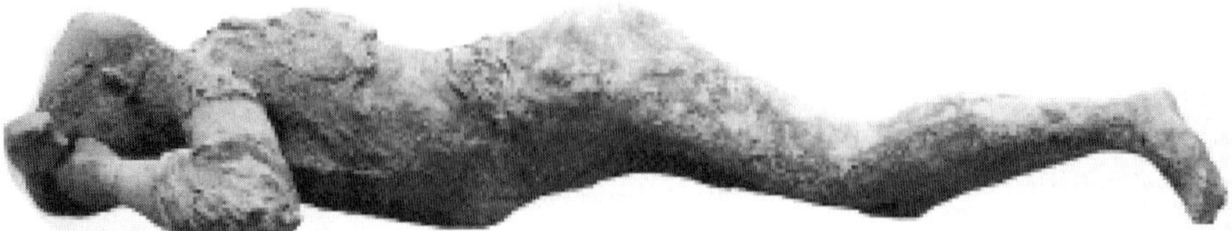

Figure 2.5 *Plaster cast of the body of a young woman, original in the Antiquarium, Pompeii. (Photo: Eric de Maré)*

Reading status

Roman society is often described as highly stratified and ordered. To illuminate some of the major divisions you should now read Essay Five in *Experiencing Rome*, 'Status and identity in the Roman world'.

Exercise

As you read the essay think about the types of status distinctions which may have operated at Ostia and Pompeii and how these might be detected.

Discussion

'Repopulating' the towns of Pompeii and Ostia involves a certain degree of inference drawn from evidence about social groups and relations in Rome itself and elsewhere in the empire. Essay Five explores the multiple ways in which status operated throughout the empire – how legal, ethnic, social and economic factors helped to define the individual. You probably suspect that all these aspects were likely to have been present among the populations of Pompeii and Ostia and that the towns were filled with men, women and children who were further distinguished by aspects such as citizenship, slavery, ethnicity, wealth and poverty. However, attempting to label people or place them in simple groups is unlikely to succeed. An individual's identity was often complex and far from fixed. Although it may be inappropriate to categorize people, it is still possible to ask what elements of status and individual identity were displayed at Pompeii and Ostia, how and by whom. And how can we detect such things?

There is no easy answer to this. We are forced to work with the available evidence, which in general does not capture the voices of the mass of the inhabitants of Pompeii and Ostia. We have access to few individual names and stories. Nevertheless, some of the material evidence does allow us to draw some tentative conclusions and comparisons. For example, variations in houses, their size, decor and furnishings, suggest economic differences; images of people found in portraits, wall paintings and tombs indicate distinctions of gender, age, dress or wealth. In addition there are some documentary sources, namely wax tablets and inscriptions which record people's names and relationships and may reveal aspects of legal, social and economic status.

In reading Essay Five you may have been particularly struck by the importance of legal status, especially the advantages and disadvantages associated with free birth or servitude and with citizenship or non-citizenship. How can we evaluate people in these terms? It is impossible to estimate with any accuracy what proportion of the populations of Pompeii and Ostia were free or slave. It is possible to infer, however, on the basis that both towns were part of Italy, that after the Social War the majority of free people, including many ex-slaves, were Roman citizens. This is not to say that there were no *peregrini* or freeborn non-citizens to be found in Pompeii or Ostia: people did move around the empire and many will not have died where they were born. Ostia, as a port and trade centre, may have had a substantial immigrant population. In addition, those slaves who were freed informally would not have become Roman citizens. Despite the apparent significance of legal status, the essay notes how it may rarely have been explicitly acknowledged or identified. This raises interesting issues about how the people of Pompeii and Ostia perceived themselves. Did legal distinctions matter? Was being a Roman citizen more important than being a Pompeian or an Ostian? Did money and family connections outweigh all other considerations?

Once more it is easier to pose these questions than to find the answers. But one context where it is sometimes possible to identify aspects of legal status is in nomenclature. Roman names could reveal facets of an individual's legal status such as citizenship, free birth or servitude (although by no means did they always do so). One method of learning about people and their names is through documents such as papyri and wax tablets. These are unusual discoveries but some have been recovered from Pompeii and the surrounding area. These documents give access to people and their activities, business transactions and legal disputes. The case of Petronia Iusta, mentioned in Essay Five, was recorded in a series of documents found at Herculaneum on the Bay of Naples, which was also destroyed by the eruption of Vesuvius in AD 79. This particular dispute reveals how issues of legal status could be contested and were of importance to some. A more common documentary source, however, which gives access to the inhabitants of towns such as Pompeii and Ostia is inscriptions. Inscriptions were set up in various contexts – they accompanied statues, adorned funerary monuments and were attached to public buildings. The term 'inscriptions' can also incorporate informal rather than formal public writing, such as the painted and scratched graffiti which have been preserved on the walls of Pompeii (see Lewis and Reinhold, pp.126 and 236–8). It is the names found in inscriptions which above all else confirm that in Pompeii and Ostia there were slaves and ex-slaves, citizens and non-citizens, and that in some circumstances these differences mattered.

You should now listen to audio cassette 2, band 2, 'Reading inscriptions'.

The aim of this exercise is to introduce you to various types of inscriptions and their visual and contextual elements. For the purpose of this course you are not expected to be able to read or translate Latin. The text of the inscriptions is reproduced so that you can appreciate the original appearance of the inscription and identify key elements such as names and titles.

To work through this band you will also need Illustrations 1–4 (Plates 2.29–2.32):

Illustration 1 (Plate 2.29): epitaph of Titus Flavius Verus, Ostia

Illustration 2 (Plate 2.30): dedicatory inscription from the small or covered theatre, Pompeii

Illustration 3 (Plate 2.31): funerary memorial of Publius Vesonius Phileros, Pompeii

Illustration 4 (Plate 2.32): detail of epitaph from Illustration 3

For each of the four inscriptions section (a) reproduces, as closely as possible, the original form and layout of the inscription; section (b) begins to decode the inscription by filling out any abbreviations and section (c) provides a translation. The accompanying illustrations also help to put some of the inscriptions into their wider context.

Inscription 1 (Illustration 1, Plate 2.29)

Ostia: funerary inscription, early third century AD (*Corpus Inscriptionum Latinarum* 14.167)

(a) T FLAVIO T F PAL VERO EQVITI ROMANO

(b) T(ito) FLAVIO T(iti) F(ilio) PAL(atina tribu) VERO EQVITI ROMANO

(c) To Titus Flavius Verus, son of Titus and of the Palatina voting tribe, an eques romanus [equestrian].

Exercise 1

Look carefully at Illustration 1, which shows the epitaph in context, then familiarize yourself with the three versions of the inscription given above.

Inscription 2 (Illustration 2, Plate 2.30)

Pompeii: inscription from the small or covered theatre, first century BC (*Corpus Inscriptionum Latinarum* 10.844). The theatre and inscription (together with the dedicatory inscription for the amphitheatre at Pompeii, which is reproduced in extract 2.2) can be seen in the video sequence 'Fora and public buildings' (t.c.1.07.12–1.08.02).

(a) C QVINCTIVS C F VALG
M PORCIVS M F
DVOVIR DEC DECR
THEATRVM TECTVM
FAC LOCAR EIDEMQ PROB

(b) C(aius) QVINCTIVS C(ai) F(ilius) VALG(us)
M(arcus) PORCIVS M(arci) F(ilius)
DVOVIR(i) DEC(urionum) DECR(eto)
THEATRVM TECTVM
FAC(iundum) LOCAR(unt) EIDEMQ(ue) PROB(arunt)

(c) Gaius Quinctius Valgus, son of Gaius, and Marcus Porcius, son of Marcus, duoviri, at the decree of the decurions, contracted the construction of the covered theatre and approved the work.

Exercise 2

Look carefully at Inscription 2, especially the translation.

What purpose did this inscription fulfil?

Can you identify any similarities and differences between the names which occur in Inscription 2 and the name in Inscription 1?

Inscription 3 (no illustration)

Rome: funerary inscription, second century AD (*Corpus Inscriptionum Latinarum* 6.10795)

(a)
DM
MERCVRIVS
SERVVS
VIX ANN XV
P AELIVS
TERTIVS
SERVO SVO
BMF

(b)
D(is) M(anibus)
MERCVRIVS
SERVVS
VIX(it) ANN(is) XV
P(ublius) AELIVS
TERTIVS
SERVO SVO
B(ene) M(erenti)
F(ecit)

(c) To the spirits of the departed Mercurius, a slave, who lived 15 years. Publius Aelius Tertius made it [the memorial] for his well-deserving slave.

Exercise 3

Using the translation of Inscription 3 above, briefly note what type of information the epitaph contains.

Look carefully at the names of the people involved. What does this tell us about their legal status?

Side 1 finishes after this exercise has been set. 'Reading inscriptions' continues on Side 2.

Inscription 4 (Illustrations 3 and 4, Plates 2.31 and 2.32)

Pompeii: Porta Nocera necropolis, first century AD

(a) P VESONIVS>L
PHILEROS
AVGVSTALIS
VIVOS
MONVMENTVM
FECIT SIBI ET SVIS

VESONIAE P F
PATRONAE ET

M ORFELLIO M L
FAVSTO AMICO

(b) P(ublius) VESONIVS G(aiae)* L(ibertus)/ PHILEROS AVGVSTALIS/VIVOS MONVMENTVM/FECIT SIBI ET SVIS

VESONIAE P(ubli) F(iliae)/PATRONAE ET

M(arco) ORFELLIO M(arci) L(iberto)/FAVSTO AMICO

(c) Publius Vesonius Phileros, the freedman of a woman and an Augustalis, made this monument for himself and his dependants during his lifetime. And also for Vesonia, daughter of Publius, his patroness, and Marcus Orfellius Faustus, freedman of Marcus, his friend.

(*Note that the symbol > stands in this context for Gaia, a generalized female *praenomen*. / = line end.)

Exercise 3

Read sections (a) and (b) of the inscription. What do the names suggest about the legal status of those commemorated?

Exercise 4

Look at Illustration 4. What do you notice about the way in which the word Augustalis in the second line is cut? What does this suggest?

You will come across many references to inscriptions as the course progresses. You have already looked at the *Res Gestae Divi Augusti* – the monumental epitaph composed by Augustus and set up in Rome. The speech of the emperor Claudius concerning the appointment of Gallic senators which you also studied in Block One was published as an inscription set up in Lyons. Lewis and Reinhold contains the translations of many inscriptions and you may wish to browse through this noting the different types. Remember, however, that a source book such as Lewis and Reinhold presents the inscriptions as disembodied texts – there is little sense of the original context, who would have been able to see and read the inscriptions or whether they would have been complemented by pictorial images. In the remainder of this section you will look at some further inscriptions, so try to keep these issues of context in mind. In Block Three you will encounter inscriptions composed in Greek and view them in their architectural settings. In Block Four you will work on a second inscription reading exercise, this time using the video. This focuses on some tombstones from Roman Britain but the introduction to this video explores the wider context of the Roman cemetery, and includes footage of the cemeteries of Pompeii.

Beyond legal status

Latin names could reveal important information about legal status, but this was not automatically the case. Remember, in particular, that inscriptions were not legal documents. There was no obligation to reveal all and thus the identity constructed for individuals through this medium could be subjective. Equally, the desire to reveal or include indications of legal status may have appealed more to some people than to others, and the conventions of nomenclature varied over time. Besides, the importance of legal status should not be overplayed. Look back to the section 'Evaluating status' in Essay Five and remember the warnings about placing people on some sort of hierarchical ladder on the basis of citizenship and legal status alone.

Legal status was only one aspect of an individual's status. Essay Five also stresses the significance of social and economic distinctions. That there were inequalities in wealth and social standing at Ostia and Pompeii is suggested by the range of housing, material goods, funerary memorials and so forth which have been found. Not everyone enjoyed the same standard of living. It is difficult to reconstruct the full range of economic activities within the towns, although you will explore some aspects of employment and trade below. You should be wary, however, of making direct analogies from the material evidence about the relative wealth and standing of individuals. Remember, for example, how some people, such as freed slaves, might overemphasize their material success as a form of compensation for the legal stigmas which continued to plague them. Equally, modest or restrained display among the wealthy might be regarded as the height of good taste.

One method of exploring the hierarchy of Pompeii and Ostia and distinctions based on prestige and/or wealth is once more through inscriptions and the items such as statues, public buildings and funerary monuments with which they were associated. Inscriptions are a fundamental source for how the constitution and administration of the towns were ordered. You have already seen this in inscriptions which defined people not only by name but also by means of titles, such as *eques romanus*, and by magisterial offices. At both Pompeii and Ostia inscriptions have identified two annually elected magistrates, the *duoviri*, with responsibility for judicial matters, and two lesser magistrates with the title of *aedile*, who were in charge of public buildings.

Look back to Inscription 2 in the ‘Reading inscriptions’ exercise above.

The two men who oversaw the construction of the theatre were *duoviri* or senior magistrates. The same men also constructed the Pompeian amphitheatre, but at that time they both held the office of *quinquennalis* (see extract 2.2 in the Supplementary Texts). This post was held every five years by the *duoviri* of that year and gave them censorial duties to revise the list of members of the *ordo decurionum*. This was the town council and had approximately 100 members. The administrative system in towns such as Ostia and Pompeii can be seen as parallel to that which operated in Rome. The *duoviri* performed a similar role to the Roman consuls and the *ordo decurionum* acted as the local equivalent of the Roman senate. However, in Pompeii and Ostia the adult male citizens voted the senior magistrates into office annually, whereas in Rome contested elections for consuls ceased under the emperors. The election slogans daubed on the walls of Pompeii suggest that the contests could be keenly fought.

Exercise

Look at the election notices from Pompeii in Lewis and Reinhold, pages 237–8.

What types of qualities are the candidates praised for? Who are their supporters?

Discussion

The candidates are praised for their personal qualities – they are worthy, good and upright citizens. Examples (ix) and (xi) expand on this slightly by acknowledging that the candidates have appropriate skills in dealing with legal and financial matters integral to their office. Example (vi) hints, however, at the two-way relationship between candidate and voter. The message is clear – if you support this candidate he will also support you. Those composing the notices include tradesmen, religious groups and neighbours. These groups hoped to benefit in some way by supporting a specific candidate. Some of the election slogans are, however, more tongue-in-cheek and reflect the social rather than the business and religious side of the town. The 'late drinkers' and the 'ball players' announce their candidates, although the candidate favoured by the 'petty thieves' may not have appreciated the declaration of support!

A public career demanded money. Those who were successful were expected to provide shows and amenities for the inhabitants. But even those who could not pursue a political career through lack of connections, money or legal stigmas could still order their lives according to hierarchical principles. Associations of workers (*collegia*) are attested at both Pompeii and Ostia. Note the support for candidates in the Pompeian elections voiced by the fruit dealers, goldsmiths and muleteers. Wealthy freedmen of the two towns frequently recorded their membership of the *ordo augustalis*, a group of priests of the imperial cult, which offered some compensation for their being debarred from other offices. Look back to Inscription 4 in the 'Reading inscriptions' exercise, the epitaph of Publius Vesonius Phileros, and note the emphasis that he placed on his title of Augustalis.

The information gained on the inhabitants of Pompeii and Ostia most often derives from public rather than private documents. Inscriptions were, in general, aimed at a public audience and as such they might present people in certain ways. Titles could be of fundamental importance. The men who constructed the Pompeian theatre and amphitheatre were defined by the offices they held; their exact legal status was of secondary importance. In fact, as with the men named in the election notices, legal status could be taken for granted; without citizenship and free birth they could not stand for office.

The insights gained are not only into public matters but are also biased towards the adult male citizen. This is not to say that there is no evidence for the women, children and slaves of Pompeii and Ostia. But often this evidence is mediated through male citizen terms.

Exercise

Read extract 2.3 in the Supplementary Texts, the inscription from the temple of Isis, Pompeii (Figure 2.6).

How might you account for the prominence given to this child?

Discussion

The inscription records how a six-year-old paid for the restoration of the temple of Isis after the earthquake of AD 62. For his generosity the town council made him a decurion free of charge. You should note that the standard age for admission to the *ordo* was twenty-five and it normally entailed an entrance fee. It is hard to believe that the six-year-old acted on his own initiative or appreciated the reward he was given. Instead it seems likely that the boy's actions and subsequent rewards were intended to advantage someone else. One possible explanation is that the boy's father was a freed slave who could not himself become a decurion. By contrast a freeborn son had no legal barriers against holding office. The wealthy father was able to buy his son privilege and no doubt increase his own standing in the process. Whether he was a son of a freed slave or not, it is clear that the glory of the boy's public generosity would reflect on his father and family.

In the video on the Pompeian forum you encountered another Pompeian inscription where a parent promoted her son by funding a public building. Eumachia paid for the construction of a portico with her son Marcus Numistrius Fronto (for a translation of this inscription see Lewis and Reinhold, p.369). As a woman Eumachia could not hold a post in the administration of Pompeii but some religious offices and honours were available to her. Eumachia is described as a public priestess and she associates the prestige derived from this title, and her public generosity in building the portico, with her son who one day would be able to stand for office. Moreover, despite her lack of direct political power Eumachia appears to have been an influential woman in her own right. Remember the statue at the rear of the building that was set up to her by the fullers. Eumachia may have acted as a patron to this

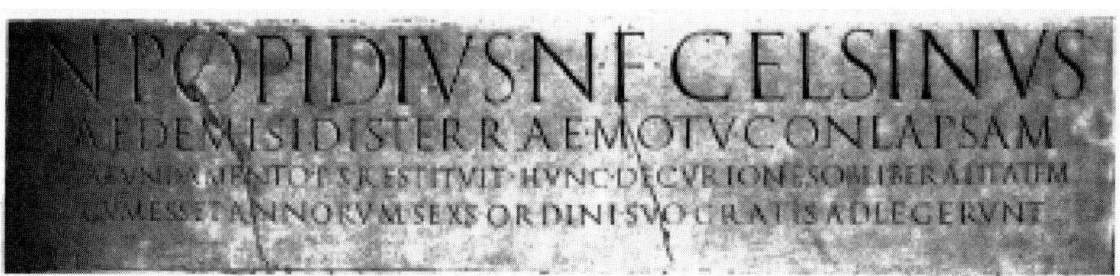

Figure 2.6 *Inscribed marble slab recording the rebuilding of the temple of Isis, Pompeii. Museo Nazionale Archeologico, Naples.*

group, a connection which one day might prove useful in the furtherance of any political aspirations of her family. Like the fruit dealers and goldsmiths, the fullers may have favoured and supported certain candidates in the Pompeian elections. At her death Eumachia received a large and impressive tomb. You will see images of this in the video sequence 'Image and text on tombstones', which you will watch in Block Four. Money and wealth appear to have given Eumachia a level of independence. Eumachia also serves as a reminder that status was a relative condition. Despite the legal restrictions confronting her, a woman could in some circumstances become more influential than her male contempories.

Roman or Pompeian?

In this section you have touched on the lives of a few individuals who lived in Ostia and Pompeii, largely through the medium of inscriptions. The insights provided are often limited to one event or action in the life (or indeed the death) of those named. But this information still provides us with valuable details on how people perceived themselves and those around them. Names in particular can be revealing. The holding of Roman citizenship, for example, was important for the privileges it entailed. On one level it would seem that the inhabitants of Pompeii and Ostia regarded themselves primarily as Roman, since this status is repeatedly declared by their nomenclature. However, it would be misleading to dismiss the importance of local identity and affiliation. Remember that when additional information was included in the inscriptions this often entailed a reference to magisterial titles or familial connections. This information was relevant on a local level; it provided distinguishing details and suggests that individual identity was defined by numerous criteria. In addition, in most cases it would be evident that those named in the inscriptions of Pompeii and Ostia were inhabitants of these places and thus further clarification was probably not required. By contrast inscriptions set up by those who were away from their native town might include a reference to where they came from. You will explore this further in Block Four when you consider epitaphs to soldiers serving in Britain that contained references to the towns and settlements from which these men originated.

To end this section we can note once more the public nature of the evidence drawn upon; in other contexts the identity displayed and constructed by the individual may have been very different. In Block Three you will watch a video sequence on houses and this includes a section based on evidence from Pompeii. This will provide an additional perspective on the lives of the inhabitants of the town. In particular it contrasts with much of the evidence already considered by focusing on home rather than public life.

2.4 Economic activity in Pompeii

You have studied some individual Pompeians and Ostians and investigated their status and identity. Now you will consider what Pompeians actually did in Pompeii. We can't examine the full range of the Pompeians' activities, so we will look at some of the basic ones, particularly how they made a living and some of the economic enterprises they engaged in. In this section we will study in some detail the evidence from excavations for economic activity in Pompeii and look at some of the people involved. It will not be possible to explore all the evidence from Pompeii in order to create a comprehensive review of the economy of Pompeii, so we will focus on selected topics which will provide an impression of the diversity of activity in the city. We will start with what at first might seem to be an unlikely part of the city – a vineyard and some gardens. We will then move off to the town centre and have a look for economic activity in and around the forum. From here we will go on to investigate textile production in the city. In the final part of this section we will briefly move to Ostia and see how that city functioned in terms of trade routes linking Rome to the empire.

Visiting Pompeii nowadays, or watching the video sequences about it, one is most struck by the surviving walls of the buildings. Generally archaeological research has concentrated on these buildings and also on the roads, which are the most durable parts of a city. This has helped to build up an image of the ancient city as a densely built-up and compact settlement. But at Pompeii, the special circumstances of its destruction have also preserved parts of the city which were not built on. Some of these were gardens. In a block of the city near the amphitheatre (Region II, Insula 2 – find it on the A2 site plan of Pompeii), two houses front the main east–west road, the Via dell'Abbondanza. One of these belonged to D. Octavius Quartio. Behind the houses a large garden occupies the remainder of the block. The garden (Jashemski, 1979, pp.45–6) has a long canal with fountains, statues and dining areas and seems to have been a pleasure garden. Other areas of the city were put to a more practical use.

At the east end of the city right next to the amphitheatre an entire city block has only one small building in the north-west corner (Region II, Insula 5) (Jashemski, 1979, pp.201–18). Find it on the A2 site plan of Pompeii and locate the buildings on the detailed plan (Plate 2.33 (a), (f) and (g)). This area was carefully excavated and found to contain over 2,000 cavities in the old land surface (black dots on Plate 2.33). Cement was poured into these cavities and when set the cast was dug out and the cavities were identified as the remains of plant roots. Most of the cavities, which lay in orderly rows four Roman feet apart, were vine roots. Alongside the vine roots were stake holes used to provide support for the vines. Scattered throughout the vineyard and especially around the edges and along the paths were other trees (open circles and black circles on Plate 2.33). These could not be identified, but Columella recommends that the fig, pear and apple should be grown in vineyards (*On Agriculture* 3.xxi, xi). An olive stone found preserved in the vineyard suggests that an olive tree may have grown there. These trees may have been used as supports for the vines to grow up but they would also have produced shade for the vines; as a bonus they may also have provided fruit or nuts.

In the partially excavated building at the north-west corner of the vineyard (Plate 2.33 (a)) one room contained the remains of a wine press and another had ten large ceramic vessels (*dolia*) set into the floor for fermenting and storing up to 12,375 litres of wine (Plate 2.33 (f) and (g)) (Jashemski 1979, pp.226–7). The other side of the building faced onto the Via dell'Abbondanza (Plate 2.33 (h)) where there was a portico and a shop front with a bar counter and shelves. It would have been the first shop a visitor to Pompeii encountered if they had entered the city through the Sarno Gate (Plate 2.33 (i)). There is no conclusive proof, but the shop was probably a bar where the house wine was grown in the vineyard behind. Most of the main thoroughfares of the city were lined with small shops (*tabernae*) like this one, or small rooms set in the street façade of town houses, which sold all manner of goods and services to the Pompeians.

The east end of Pompeii was generally less built up than other parts closer to the centre of town, and behind another pair of houses near the amphitheatre (Region I, Insula 15) is another open area where the remains of plants were found (Plates 2.34 and 2.35) (Jashemski, 1979, pp.233–42). The house at the north-west corner (at the top of Plate 2.35) is known as the 'House of the Ship Europa' after a graffito of a ship named Europa that was found on a wall of the peristyle (courtyard). It was in a poor state of repair and being renovated at the time of the eruption; this might help to explain the pile of lava gravel (Plate 2.34 G) found in the garden. The garden is on two levels; the part nearer the house is higher and along both of the long walls are banks or ramps of higher soil (Plate 2.34 (J) and (K)). In the lower part of the garden is an L-shaped path (Plate 2.34 (L)) and two areas where trenches containing rows of root cavities were found (Plate 2.34 (D) and (E)). In the rest of the lower garden were rows of vines with scattered trees around. The walls of the garden were lined with mature trees. A number of flowerpots with holes in their sides, particularly suitable for cuttings,

Figure 2.7 *Bar in Pompeii (Region VI, Insula 10). (Photo: Alinari-Anderson)*

were also found close to the walls. The overall impression is of an intensively gardened plot containing many trees and vines. The trees were not identified but fragments of fig, hazel nuts, grape pips, almond shell, date stones and broad or horse beans were found. Two of the beans even contained the remains of weevils. Doubtless other plants which left no traces of their roots were also grown and the scale of the garden, compared with the modesty of the house, suggests that the garden was producing for the market and the people of Pompeii.

In Pompeii, just like all other Roman cities, one of the functions of the forum was to act as a focus of market activity. The open space of the forum (Plate 2.28) may have been used for market stalls and there may well have also been stalls under the colonnades around the forum. There are no direct remains of any market stalls, but on one side of the square is a slab of stone with cavities scooped out of it (Plate 2.36). It bears the inscription 'Aulus Clodius Flaccus son of Aulus and Arcaeus Arellianus Caledus son of Numerius, the two chief magistrates with judicial power, set up these standardized measures by order of the *ordo decurionum*'.

The inscription basically identifies the authorities who placed the stone there. Two Roman citizens who are magistrates are named; they have legal powers and are acting on the orders of the *ordo decurionum*. The stone is a *mensa ponderaria,* literally a measure of weight: the cavities are a set of standard measures of volume. It was used to check that goods were sold in the correct legal quantities so that people did not get short measures. The inscription implies that fair trading was overseen and ensured by the two named magistrates of the *ordo decurionum.* It is evidence for a regulated market in the forum controlled by the power of the *ordo decurionum.*

On the opposite side of the forum (see Plate 2.37) is a building known as the Macellum, a large building with a courtyard surrounded by porticoes. Here excavations found evidence in the form of fish scales in a drain at the centre of the structure. The remains of cereals and fruit were also found in the northern rooms of the structure. This evidence suggests the building was a market hall housing stalls or shops selling provisions and the central structure was a set of permanent stalls for selling fish. This likely interpretation provides evidence for economic exchange taking place by the side of the forum.

Further along the same side of the forum is the large building known as the Eumachia building (Plate 2.38) which you have studied in the 'Fora and public buildings' video sequence. The statue of a woman found there bore an inscription which read 'Eumachia daughter of Lucius, public priestess, set up by the fullers' (Plate 2.49). Fullers washed and prepared wool and also cloth. This inscription, where Eumachia is honoured by a group of wool workers, has been used to suggest that the building was some kind of wool exchange or market. Although the corridor (a covered gallery) which runs around the outside of the building could have provided useful secure storage space, there is no strong evidence to link the building with the wool trade other than the statue dedicated by the fullers. But who were these people and what did they do? To answer this question we need to find more evidence for their activities at Pompeii.

A house (IX.13.5) belonging to Fabius Ululutremulus further along the Via dell'Abbondanza had several graffiti scratched on the walls. One of the workers there is described as an '*atramentarius*', literally one who dyed things black. Some paintings on these walls depict Aeneas fleeing from Troy with Anchises and his son Ascanius, while another shows Romulus. The Virgilian theme continues in a graffito which parodies the first line of the Aeneid: '*Fullones ululamque cano, non arma virumque*', 'I sing of the fullers and the owl, not of arms and the man'. The owl referred to is the companion of the goddess Minerva, the protector of fullers. The owl also appears in the second name of the owner of the establishment, Ululutremulus, which can be translated as 'Owl fearer'. The names of five slaves who worked here are also known from graffiti: Sula, Calamus, Pegte, Ricinus and Gerulus. Only the front of this building has been excavated so it does not provide further detailed evidence for fulling.

Figure 2.8 *Copy of a wall painting of a bread shop from Pompeii, house VII.3.30. Museo della Civiltà Romana, Rome, original in the Museo Nazionale Archeologico, Naples. (Photo: Phil Perkins)*

Exercise

Look closely at Plate 2.39. This wall painting is from the very grand 'House of the Vettii' in Pompeii. It is one of a sequence of friezes from the same room which show little cupids engaged in various forms of sport and industry. Other panels show the manufacture of perfume, goldsmithing, baking and wine making. Try to identify the activities the figures in the wall painting are doing. Jot them down.

Discussion

This panel shows cupids working with cloth. On the left two cupids are treading cloth in a vat. This may be to wash it or to thicken or felt it. By their side are two amphorae which may contain fuller's earth (a hydrous aluminium silicate used for cleaning, which was transported from the island of Ponza to Pompeii) or urine, which was also used in the fulling process. In the centre the cupids are combing cloth (it's hard to tell what one is doing). The figures towards the right are holding the cloth up to the light, possibly to check its cleanliness or its even texture. One of the cupids is carefully folding up some cloth. (What is the last figure up to?)

Exercise

Do you think the picture of cloth-working cupids (Plate 2.39) is a dependable piece of evidence for how cloth was worked in Pompeii? Give your reasons.

Discussion

The picture is obviously not recording real life because the workers are cupids not people. Nevertheless, the activities are carefully represented in some detail and may even work in a sequence from washing to combing to checking to folding away, outlining one of the processes we might expect to find in a cloth workshop. Although the activities are set in an imaginary world they do provide useful indications of what work the cloth workers would have done. The image also provides a reminder of the details and intricacy of cloth working. Some of these activities, such as folding and checking cloth, would be hard to detect in any other way because they leave no traces, while others such as washing cloth in a trough might be detectable by examining a workshop such as Fabius Ululutremulus' house. So although the pictures do not show the workings of an actual workshop nor the physical arrangement of one, they do provide an indication of the kinds of activities that would have taken place.

Many tanks and vats have been found in buildings at Pompeii. In some cases old houses were converted into workshops full of vats, but one large establishment was purpose built. A few blocks from Ululutremulus' house towards the forum and on the other side of the same road is a large building (Plates 2.40 and 2.41), on the front wall of which are painted some political graffiti similar to those you studied in section 2.3. One reads 'Stephanus supports ...' while another reads 'The United Fullers support ...', and because of these graffiti the building is known as the '*fullonica* of Stephanus' (*fullonica* is Latin for a fuller's workshop). When the building was excavated in 1911 the wide front door was ajar and in the room (a) just inside a skeleton was found on the floor. There were 1,089 *sestertii* in gold, silver and bronze coin next to the skeleton. It cost one *denarius* (four *sestertii*) to clean a tunic, so that sum represents maybe 250 cleaned items. The skeleton is unidentified: the money could be the day's takings but could equally well be the booty of a looter overcome in the eruption of Vesuvius. To the left of the door (see Plate 2.41) was a press, to the right was a small room, possibly for receiving customers, and straight ahead was an open courtyard or atrium containing an open water tank (c). The atrium is unlike normal domestic atria, which have pitched roofs. This one has a flat roof, which could have been used for drying or sun-bleaching cloth or clothes. On the far side of this were two more rooms; nothing was found to suggest a function but one of the rooms also had a door opening on the far side towards the back of the house. Also next to the atrium is a room (d) with red walls decorated with two flying figures representing Summer and Autumn. Between this and the entrance was a small windowless room (e) of uncertain use but possibly a store. From the red room a corridor led to a small garden surrounded by columns (peristyle). On the far side of the peristyle (g) are three large tanks (h) connected by pipes for soaking or washing; a walkway runs along these to allow access and steps lead into the tanks. On either side of these are some basins for pounding cloth and some containers to store urine. Off the corner of the garden is a small kitchen (i) where a set of pans was found on the hob and a barbecue on a tripod hanging on the wall. This is where the workers' meals would have been prepared. Next to this was a toilet (j). On the other side of the garden a stair led up to the roof terrace. These remains provide direct evidence for the workings of a *fullonica*. However, we still have limited information about what was actually washed. Was it only new cloth or did the place also work as a launderette? We can really only speculate about precisely how the various tanks were used, but images like the wall paintings of the cupids (Plate 2.39) give us some idea of the activities that would have taken place in this workshop.

There were at least twenty-three fullers' workshops, five weaving shops, six dye works, four felt works and a wool-processing workshop in Pompeii, but how important were they in economic terms? And did the owners have any economic power? Some scholars have suggested that the textile industry was the most important in Pompeii because of the number of workshops and also because of the link between the Eumachia building and the statue of her presented by the fullers. However, that statue is the only known link between Eumachia, the building and the fullers. Furthermore, it is not conclusive evidence: another graffito from the building mentions the silversmiths, for example, and the building clearly has connections with imperial power. Of the people certainly known to be connected with the textile industry most are freedmen or slaves. The names of two high-status individuals, Lucius Veranius Hypsaeus and Marcus Vesonius Primus, have been linked with fullers' premises, but the evidence is weak (Jongman, 1988, pp.172–5). It seems that the highest ranks of local society, magistrates (such as *duoviri*), were not reached by fullers themselves. However, the graffiti from the front of the *fullonica* of Stephanus do suggest that the fullers were an organized group, and they may have had political influence through the voting power of their organization. Overall we know little about the ownership and economic value of the fullers' workshops. One is known to have belonged to the city of Pompeii and have been rented by Lucius Caecilius Jucundus for the sum of 1,652 *sestertii* a year (= 415 dry-cleaned tunics). Jucundus was a banker, an auctioneer and a tax farmer, so he probably did not run the business himself. Presumably he had a freedman or slave to run it. We know about this rental because part of the business archive of Jucundus was discovered on 154 wax tablets in his house in Pompeii. These record transactions between AD 52 and 62 and the average size of each transaction was 8,502 *sestertii*, so the rental for the premises was not large when compared with the range of deals Jucundus was involved in. Other industry in the city can be directly connected to leaders of society, for example the magistrate A. Umbricius Scaurus, and the names of some of his freedmen were found stamped on amphorae used in a fish sauce factory, suggesting that he owned it. However, we do not really have enough evidence to decide how important these manufacturing industries were in Pompeii. The wealthier members of society may well have derived their income from other sources, such as agricultural estates and money lending, but at Pompeii the clearest evidence relates to small-scale manufacture and processing of agricultural produce such as wool or grapes, which took place within the city and was thoroughly integrated with the housing and public buildings of the city.

Cities in the wider economy

Pompeii was a small town in Campania and most of the economic activity we can see there is related to agriculture, processing of produce, retailing and small-scale manufacture of items for use in and around the city. This is likely to be typical of most towns in Italy. Nevertheless, some towns, such as Nola close to Pompeii, did gain a reputation for producing specialities: Cato tells us that Nola was the place to buy copper pans (*On Agriculture* 135), although we don't know how important these specialities were in the local economy. There is little firm evidence to suggest that Pompeii produced large quantities of goods or specialities to be traded to other parts of the Roman empire. Ostia, on the other hand, performed a pivotal role in the economy of both the empire and the city of Rome. As we have noted above, during the first century AD Ostia developed from a small town at the mouth of the Tiber into a sprawling port acting as a vital link between Rome and the empire.

Ostia played a central role as an entrepôt between Rome and the empire. This function contributed to the development of the city and explains why there are so many warehouses, shops and offices in the city of Ostia. The city does have many typical features of a Roman city, as you have discovered earlier in the block, but its special position and role led to the development of these additional features.

In this section you have seen how economic activity was a part of the life of Pompeians and also how it contributed to the urban fabric of the city, with cultivated areas, markets, shops and workshops. This is also true of Ostia, but here the city's specific role led to exaggerated development of commercial facilities. In many ways Ostia was the gateway between Rome and the empire and goods flowed through it from all over the empire (Block Five explores this further). In the next part of the block you will investigate how this exposure to the empire affected Rome and Italy.

Part Three: Romans and Italians

BY VALERIE HOPE, CHRIS EMLYN-JONES, PAULA JAMES AND PHIL PERKINS

In Part Three of this block you will explore the relationship between Rome and Italy and how this was affected by the acquisition of empire. Central to this will be the acknowledgement of both the positive and negative sides of the empire. In a literary case study you will assess how the empire's impact on Rome encouraged some writers to re-evaluate their rural Italian roots. You will also look beyond this rhetoric to consider how the empire affected the economy of Rome and Italy in practice. In short, how did the empire alter perceptions of both Rome and Italy and redefine Roman identity?

3.1 *Luxuria* and the corruption of Italy

The empire brought many advantages to Rome and Italy but there was also a sense, as reflected in contemporary literature, that the empire changed Rome and Italy for the worse rather than the better. Things which flooded in from the provinces, whether people, religions or material goods, altered the very definition of Roman identity and, to some contemporary observers, threatened to destroy it for ever. Here we want to focus on an aspect that caused frequent concern to Roman traditionalists: *luxuria*, or the wanton display of wealth. The empire made Rome and individual Romans wealthy; there was nothing wrong with money and the accumulation of money, but how it should be spent could be a bone of contention. Concerns were voiced throughout the late republic and imperial periods that money and wealth corrupted and wanton display was very un-Roman. The ideal persisted that wealth was limited in Rome's not-so-distant past and in those good old days the Roman ancestors worked the family farm with their own hands; life was austere and personal interest was subsumed to the interests of the state.

The work in this section will involve reading some extracts from Lewis and Reinhold and the Supplementary Texts.

The advent of *luxuria*

To introduce the advent of *luxuria* in Rome you should now read extracts 2.5 and 2.6 in the Supplementary Texts and the extract from Seneca's *Moral Epistles* on pages 156–7 of Lewis and Reinhold.

Exercise

As you read the passages consider what types of behaviour were admired and what types of behaviour were questioned.

Discussion

The extracts originate from diverse types of literature, but all three authors were writing during the imperial period, and all three look back on the past through rose-tinted spectacles. This is most apparent in the passage from Seneca, where he contrasts the simple lifestyle of Scipio Africanus with what he sees as the decadence of his own day. Scipio lived simply; he worked the fields with his own hands, his house was poor and the bathing facilities were limited. By contrast the baths of Seneca's day were extremely luxurious, full of mirrors, marble, mosaics, glass, silver, statues and precious stones. Note in particular how the baths were decorated with the riches of empire – Alexandrian and Thasian marble and Numidian stone. The passage by Pliny the Elder is an attempt to trace the arrival of such luxuries in Rome. The highlighting of certain dates may be somewhat schematic, but the message is clear – conquest and the empire brought both extravagant goods and the display of and competition for these items. Pliny uses strong language to express what he perceives to be the negative consequences of this taste for *luxuria.* He speaks of a 'blow to our morals'; he describes the disappearance of scruples in the desire to buy precious items; and he suggests that the people began 'to covet foreign opulence'. Livy, who was writing in the time of Augustus, also describes the impact of *luxuria* in Rome of the second century BC. In his histories of early Rome Livy incorporates a speech, purportedly made by Cato the Elder in 195 BC, against the repeal of a law which controlled expenditure and display of costly items. Cato the Elder (234–149 BC), a senator and distinguished politician, had a reputation for being concerned that Rome would be undermined and corrupted by the empire. Here Livy has him speak of 'avarice and extravagance' and warns against the 'sensual allurements' of the east. In Cato's opinion (and probably Livy's too – note extract 2.4, which is taken from the beginning of Livy's work) people had become more interested in foreign goods and luxuries than they were in traditional Roman values and religion.

The passages emphasize the simplicity and honesty of the rural lifestyle and this ideal was contrasted with the evils and corruption of city life. You will explore this rhetorical contrast, specifically in relation to poetry and satire, in the next section. The idea of the corruption of Rome was, however, a common literary motif throughout the history of Latin literature. But the critique of luxury was more than a literary theme.

Politicians such as Cato appear to have genuinely believed that increasing *luxuria* would mark the fall of Rome and took action accordingly. During the republic, for example, legislation, often termed sumptuary laws, was introduced to curtail expenditure on luxury goods. Such legislation normally failed as the wealthy moved on to new forms of extravagant expenditure. Cato had been particularly vociferous in his criticisms of the influence of Greek culture. Note as well how Pliny the Elder pinpoints the acquisition of Asia and Achaia (Greece) as the moments when Rome was exposed to extravagant living. Despite these criticisms Rome found much to admire in Greece, Asia and the east: the art, philosophy and religion of these areas made a marked impact in Rome. Books, libraries, art, statues, philosophers, teachers and artisans were imported from Greece into Rome and Italy. The opulence and indulgence of this culture contrasted with Roman traditionalism, and this could lead to conflict and criticism. Hence Cato's comment that Rome itself was at risk of becoming a captive. For further discussion of the influences of Greek culture on Rome you should refer to Essay Four in *Experiencing Rome*. The general theme will also be explored in Block Three.

Controlling *luxuria*

By the time of Augustus the prizes of empire had flowed into Italy and the élite had become accustomed to displaying their wealth. Money became all-important in the final years of the republic; it was a means of buying support and impressing the masses. Nevertheless, the ideal image of the hard-working unostentatious Roman (or perhaps more accurately Italian) persisted. At the beginning of his *History of Rome* Livy, who wrote during the time of Augustus, praises the Roman ancestors and emphasizes their thrift, plain living and poverty (extract 2.4). But he contrasts this with the avarice, luxury and moral decline present in his own day. Through these words Livy reveals the standpoint that will influence the shape of his narrative. As you have already seen, the sentiments that Livy gives to Cato the Elder in extract 2.5 would appear to parallel his own. But debates about morality and *luxuria* could have a serious political content, which in turn provided the backdrop for writers such as Livy. In particular, think of Octavian's propaganda campaign against Antony. Octavian presented himself as a traditional Roman, whereas Antony was portrayed as living a life of opulence and extravagance in the east and getting up to some very un-Roman activities. After the battle of Actium Augustus had to live up to the image he had created for himself. Indeed, his claim to have restored the republic encompassed a return to traditional Roman ways (ways that were much admired and promoted by contemporary authors such as

Livy). Remember from Block One how Augustus conducted himself with modesty and created a caring and simple image for himself. It also needs to be noted that advocating traditional values may have been a useful mechanism employed by Augustus to protect himself from ambitious rivals. Augustus created an environment where it was no longer acceptable for members of the élite to live extravagantly and court popularity through flamboyant behaviour. Augustus led by example. Suetonius suggests that Augustus disliked large and pretentious houses and actually demolished a villa built by his granddaughter on too lavish a scale (Suetonius, *Augustus* 72). When Vedius Pollio (a wealthy supporter of Augustus) died he bequeathed his Roman mansion, which Ovid described as 'larger than many a small city' (Ovid, *Fasti* 6.642), to the emperor. Augustus promptly had the house demolished and restored the land to public use (Cassius Dio, *Roman History* 54.23.1–6), thus turning private property into public property. Augustus' own example was probably underpinned by legislation or sumptuary laws to control extravagant expenditure, although the precise details of these remain unclear.

Exercise

Now read Lewis and Reinhold, sections 43 and 44, pages 155–62.

Think about the acceptable and unacceptable sides of *luxuria* and mechanisms for its control.

Discussion

Augustus' legislation did not succeed in stopping the Roman love for luxurious living. In the first passage (pp.155–6) Tacitus recalls how extravagance became an issue once more under Tiberius and how the latter called for modesty and, like many before him, recalled the self-control of previous generations. Indeed, the ideal of modesty and decorum also persisted. For the élite it was perhaps possible, at least in theory, to marry these two seemingly opposing viewpoints. Wealth and luxury were part of the senatorial lifestyle – *luxuria* defined the social status of the senator. In the political redundancy of the early empire *luxuria* also provided an outlet for competition and the construction of a reputation. Yet there were unwritten rules about levels of acceptable display. Those who broke them, whether by buying expensive furniture or covering themselves with jewels (pp.157–8), could expect to be condemned. The ideal was to invest in land, not in fineries and fripperies. Note how in the last extract (pp.160–2) Pliny's villa, a large complex of rooms with its own suite of baths, is described as 'a little villa', spacious enough for his needs and inexpensive to run. Pliny boasts about his property, but in terms of its practicalities, serenity and modesty rather than its extravagance. A senator's villa was designed to impress, but it should not cross the line into opulence. But the high life also appealed to the *nouveaux riches*, and their ignorance of the rules of polite society and the right and wrong ways to spend money could turn them into objects of scorn and satire. Note how Seneca saves his most condemning remarks about the luxuries of contemporary baths for those belonging to wealthy freedmen which cross all the bounds of modesty (p.157). Freedmen, by virtue of their birth, lacked breeding in the eyes of their social betters. Trimalchio, the literary creation of Petronius (pp.158–60), is the ultimate parody of the rich freedman who aims to impress but represents the epitome of bad taste (see Essay Four). The dinner party he holds entails vast expense and numerous tricks and delicacies to impress his guests. This is *luxuria* taken to the extreme.

Once more, you may have noted the inherent contrast between the city of Rome on the one hand and the Italian countryside on the other. For example, Pliny can escape from the city to his country villa, from where he describes his absent friend as 'citified'. There is, however, a certain irony that in escaping to the countryside many of the trappings of the city accompanied the wealthy. The country villas of the well-to-do were like small towns which supplied all the necessary comforts of life. Indulging in the rural idyll did not entail a return to peasant living. Nevertheless, extravagance and its associated evils were regarded as the preserve of city life. It is worth noting that such corruption was not always confined to Rome. The great feast of the freed slave Trimalchio does not appear to have been set in Rome. Puteoli or one of the important trade towns of coastal Italy is a more probable backdrop for the acquisition and display of Trimlachio's fortune. Italy was not immune to the corruptions of empire.

Luxuria was both indulged in and condemned, often, it would seem, by the same people. On one level this smacks of hypocrisy, of saying one thing and doing another, and of élite codes of behaviour designed to expose the uninitiated. But to say this would be to underplay the importance of expected and acceptable behaviour in terms of the construction of Roman identity. This is perhaps most apparent in the ambiguous attitude towards Greek culture. Antony was depicted as weakened and almost feminized by his exposure to the luxuries of the east. Augustus deliberately distanced himself from such influences in public, but this did not mean that he abandoned all things Greek. He employed Greek teachers (Cassius Dio, *Roman History* 51.16.4, 56.43.2); and a Greek supervised the imperial libraries and served as a procurator in Asia (Strabo, *Geography* 618). This was not hypocrisy but the challenge of empire: to take what was wanted from the vast and diverse territories, whether luxury or learning, while retaining that elusive quality of *romanitas.*

3.2 Portraiture in Roman Italy

An area that illustrates the fusion of things Greek and Roman is portraiture. Portraits, whether statues, relief carvings or images on coins, were concerned not just with recording people's appearances but also with how people saw themselves and wished to be seen by others. This idea was introduced in Block One when you considered some portraits of the emperor Augustus. Remember how these contributed to and propagated the emperor's chosen image. An element of such self-presentation was the fusing of cultural traits, which was often unconscious but sometimes deliberate. Roman portraiture was heavily influenced by Greek and Hellenistic models. But the tradition of commemorating people through images was also a long-established custom in Rome and Italy. The fusion of Greek and Roman traditions was not always seamless, especially during the late republic. Cato the Elder, whom you encountered above as a critic of luxury, condemned the use of extravagant statues in Rome (Plutarch, *Life of Cato the Elder* 19). Traditional honorary statues of Greek kings and heroes which depicted them naked may have seemed particularly out of place in a Roman setting. With time a greater harmony between the Greek and Roman portrait tradition was achieved, but this did not necessarily mean that there was uniformity in details of execution or that there was a single 'Roman' approach towards portraiture.

In this section you will consider the interplay between the different cultural traits – Greek, Roman and Italian – by evaluating a series of portraits from Rome and Italy which date from the late republic to the mid second century AD. You will need to have the Illustrations Book to hand and you will be guided through the portraits on an audio cassette. You will be looking at some major developments in the art of portrait sculpture in Roman Italy at this time, especially in terms of the course themes of culture, identity and power.

As you work through this exercise remember to keep the subject matter of the previous section in mind – especially the concept of *luxuria* and the moral dialogue about acceptable and unacceptable behaviour. The use and nature of portraiture could raise moral issues – not just about Roman versus Greek identity but also about the manipulation of certain qualities and characteristics. A portrait was a pictorial means of communication commissioned to create a certain impression. Once more, remember the timeless, handsome face of Augustus and the messages that could be conveyed by dress, whether that of the soldier or the priest. This idealization in personal presentation was not just confined to those who can be loosely described as the powerful or the élite. Many people aspired to be commemorated in a lasting fashion that would make a statement to the world about who they were and what they had achieved.

For this exercise you will need audio cassette 1, band 3, 'Portraiture' and Illustrations 1–10:

Illustration 1 (Plate 2.42): statue of a general from Tivoli

Illustration 2 (Plate 2.43): portrait head of Pompey the Great

Illustration 3 (Plate 2.44): head of Augustus (the complete statue is shown in Plate 1.2)

Illustration 4 (Plate 2.45): man holding two portrait busts

Illustration 5 (Plate 2.46): funerary relief of Lucius Ampudius Philomusus

Illustration 6 (Plate 2.47): cuirassed statue of Marcus Holconius Rufus

Illustration 7 (Plate 2.48): portrait head of Lucius Caecilius Felix

Illustration 8 (Plate 2.49): statue of Eumachia

Illustration 9 (Plate 2.50): sarcophagus of Gaius Junius Euhodus and Metilia Acte

Illustration 10 (Plate 2.51): relief of a vegetable seller

You will hear the Latin terms *virtus, auctoritas* and *gravitas* used to describe particular Roman social values, which are probably best translated as courage, authority and moral seriousness. Reference is made to Cato's attitude to portraits; the ancient source for this is Plutarch, *Life of Cato the Elder* 19. Ancient sources for the use of funerary and other types of portraits are Polybius, *History* 6.53; Pliny, *Natural History* 35.6–7.

Also mentioned are two particular periods of Greek art: the 'classical' period of the fifth century BC, in which people were shown in ideal, often rather generic, terms, and the 'Hellenistic' period (roughly from the late fourth century to the mid first century BC), in which there was greater interest in the individual in terms of status and personality.

Eumachia (Illustration 8) and her building have been mentioned earlier, in sections 2.3 and 2.4; the building, now containing a copy of this statue, can be seen in the video section on the Pompeian forum (t.c.1:12:35–1:14.31).

Now listen to band 3 of audio cassette 1.

3.3 Rural Italy – poetic attitudes

In studying the contribution of Roman poetry to our understanding of Italy in the empire, we will not be trawling it for literal evidence even if we focus on descriptions of the countryside, agricultural practices or rustic meals. We could easily take such descriptions at face value: Virgil's didactic poem *Georgics* and Juvenal's *Satires* are full of such detail. Yet the bald conveying of such information is not these poets' only intention, or even their primary one. You have already seen in Block One that Virgil, Horace and Propertius did not so much describe the battle of Actium as use it as a key image to convey their own perceptions, values and feelings about the emergence of Augustus and what he stood for. Indeed, as you have seen in Block One, Italy as a patriotic image plays a key role in the poetic recreation of Actium, and as one side of a polarity – Italy's gods facing outlandish Egyptian deities ('Barking Anubis' opposed to Neptune, Venus and Minerva in Virgil, *Aeneid* 8.698) (extract 1.1) and Italian celebratory wine, 'Caecuban', as opposed to foreign 'Mareotic' (Horace, *Odes* 1.37.5 and 14) (extract 1.3).

In this section of Block Two we will be exploring these and other images of Italy in the works of the Roman poets, starting briefly with Virgil and Horace again, but then moving to look in more detail at an important poet who lived later in the empire, the satirist Juvenal. We will be particularly concerned with what these poets convey about Roman perceptions of their own culture and identity at different stages of the development of their relationship with Italy.

Introduction: images of Italy in Virgil and Horace

There has been plenty of evidence that the Roman image of Italy was not invented by poets. Augustus sought to use the resonances of 'Italy' to give his regime authenticity and broad appeal through a variety of media (see Block One on the *Res Gestae* and Ara Pacis). In doing so he sought to suppress or exploit tensions arising from historical reality (the relatively recent, and not bloodless, incorporation of the Italian cities into the Roman state: see section 1.1 of this block) and economic reality (the depredations left by civil war). Virgil and Horace both reflected and used these tensions, perhaps more acutely in that they were both non-Romans in the strict sense: Virgil came from Mantua, an area which until its incorporation into Italy was part of Cisalpine Gaul (which you have studied in section 1.2), while Horace came originally from Venusia, a town which had been prominently anti-Rome in the Social War of 91–87 BC.

The definition of Italy, in direct contrast with other images, is particularly prominent in a passage of Virgil – *Georgics* 2.136–76.

Exercise

Please read this passage now in extract 2.7. In the discussion we will seek to (1) establish what the various details of the passage refer to, and then (2) consider their broader significance.

Discussion

1 At this point in the poem, Virgil suddenly interrupts a complex discussion of vines and arboriculture to embark on a panegyric of Italy, a distinct section within the construction of Book 2 of the *Georgics*. Discussion of exotic trees leads into a variety of comparisons. We first learn what Italy does *not* have: the rich gold and spices or other evocations of the east ('Median' – Persian, 'Ganges', 'Hermus' – a river of Asia Minor, 'Bactra' – a region of Parthia, 'Indies', 'Arabia', lines 136–9 – all places with rich, exotic resonances) or a time-honoured mythological past (the Greek myth in which armed men sprang from a ploughed field alluded to in lines 140–2). Its assets are rich crops, fertile livestock, metals, a favourable climate and an absence of wild beasts and poisonous weeds (lines 143–4, 149–54, 165). Moreover, to complete this guidebook Utopia, lines 155–7 convey a distinctive image of 'noble cities' (*egregias urbes*) placed on steep crags above peacefully gliding rivers.

The other dimension of this picture is Rome. Italy produces horses for battle (line 145, 'charger': *bellator equus*) and also special animal victims for military triumphs (lines 146–7, 'victim': *victima*, animal for sacrifice and 'holy water': *flumine sacro*, both emphasize the religious aspect of the description; Clitumnus was a river in Umbria, in the pastures of which were fed the white horses reserved for the religious ceremonies). Italy is also the site of Julius Caesar's and Agrippa's marine engineering works (the point of the Italian geographical allusions in lines 158–64: in 37 BC Agrippa had joined the Lucrine and Avernian lakes to make the Portus Iulius). Italy also produces hardy peoples who contribute to the Roman war effort, keeping Rome's enemies at bay and possessing the distinction of having produced many of Rome's war heroes, including Augustus himself (lines 167–76). The passage concludes climactically with an invocation to Italy as the 'land of Saturn' (*Saturnia Tellus*) – Saturn was an ancient Roman god of the countryside.

2 On the surface this passage is Virgil's justification, as he says (lines 174–6), for devoting a major poem to such a subject ('sing

a rural theme throughout the cities of Rome'). Yet Italy is also quite carefully placed in a plurality of contexts: a 'golden age' of hardy austerity and simplicity which, by implication, produces material plenty – a situation that extends into the present as an object lesson for Rome, and which can be contrasted with the exotic luxurious east. At the same time Italy represents the basis, in religious and military terms, of Roman imperial success, both in the past (Decii, Marii, Camilli, Scipios – famous republican military families, lines 169–70) and the present (Augustus and, by allusion, Julius Caesar and Agrippa, lines 163, 170–1). The passage is carefully arranged to reach a climax with the rural aspect ('land of Saturn') which has strong resonances with the past and agriculture (and Saturn was exclusively Roman). Yet the triumphant victory over craven distant enemies (line 172: 'war-worthless Indians'), only four lines earlier, still echoes. Is this imperial theme also part of *Saturnia Tellus*?

In this poem, as opposed to the image of Actium as discussed in Block One, we have a *three-way* split: Rome/Italy/the empire. Yet Virgil seems to be trying to assimilate Italy to Rome by emphasizing their common purpose against their non-Italian enemies. Moreover, each image contributes to the other: Rome acquires, by implication, the Italian rural Utopia, but also the hardy, even ruthless, soldiers, nurtured in austere simplicity, who enable the Romans (Rome-plus-Italy) to conquer an empire – an effective counter-image to ennervating 'eastern' *luxuria* – while Italy shares in the imperial victories and triumphs of Rome.

Here Virgil succeeds in uniting the tension, one might almost say the contradiction, of imperial war and rustic peace, by appealing to carefully placed images of great potency for Roman readers – images which, we have already seen, reached a much wider audience through other media. In this assimilation, which was an essential part of legitimizing the Augustan regime, poets such as Virgil both reflected and created 'Italy', a place which did not exist, and had indeed never existed in the form it was presented, but which was not completely fictitious either: the *Georgics* testify to Virgil's close detailed knowledge of the Italian countryside coupled with the improbable but powerful projection of rural values on to an imperial agenda. The passage powerfully conveys how essential 'Italy' was for the consciousness of a Roman identity.

(As Colour Plate 2.1 illustrates, contemporary wall paintings in the houses of the élite also presented this theme of the rural idyll through dreamy landscapes and rustic vistas.)

Exercise

In the light of this discussion please now read another passage from the *Georgics*: 2.490–542, extract 2.8 in the Supplementary Texts. While reading, consider (1) what kind of images characterize Rome and Italy here, and (2) how they are related.

Discussion

1. On each side of the polarity, Virgil chooses images which conjure up the city way of life: the fasces (bundles of rods which symbolized a magistrate's authority) (line 495), public records (line 502), riches (lines 506–7), civil war (line 496), versus the fruitful annual farming round (lines 513–22), simple pleasures enjoyed in loving country households (lines 523–31) and peace (lines 538–40), the latter being associated with Italian peoples in 'days of old' (lines 532, 534) and originally Rome itself ('Remus and his brother', line 533).
2. Far from being allies as in the previous piece, Rome and Italy here represent opposed ways of life couched in morally polar terms: the city is totally negative and destructive; the countryside entirely positive: idyllic and physically and morally fruitful. Lines 532–40 introduce a further potent idea: the recreation of the past as morally superior to the present. The annual labour of line 514, as opposed to corrupt life in the city or the unpleasantness of life on the outposts of the empire, is projected back as a lost way of country life from which Rome has been separated by *luxuria*, war and empire.

Virgil recited the *Georgics* to Octavian (soon to become Augustus) shortly after the battle of Actium in 31 BC (Suetonius, *Life of Virgil* 27). At about the same time Horace wrote *Satires* 2.6 (extract 2.9), in which he contrasts the city life of Rome with the countryside using the potent image of his 'Sabine farm', a small estate among the Sabine hills to the north-east of Tivoli, which had been given to him by his patron, and Augustus' minister, Maecenas. The moral fulfilment of the simple life in the countryside (see extract 2.8 above) is here coupled with a further powerful image for the Roman, that of *otium*, 'leisure', 'getting away from it all', using the countryside as a refuge from the (exaggerated?) busyness and unpleasantness of life in the city. Uncoupled from *labor* (Horace does not actually do much work himself on his estate), the countryside represents peace, safety, independence and the simple life. This strongly positive picture of the countryside resembles that of Virgil in extract 2.8 in the values it places on town and country, but at a personal level.

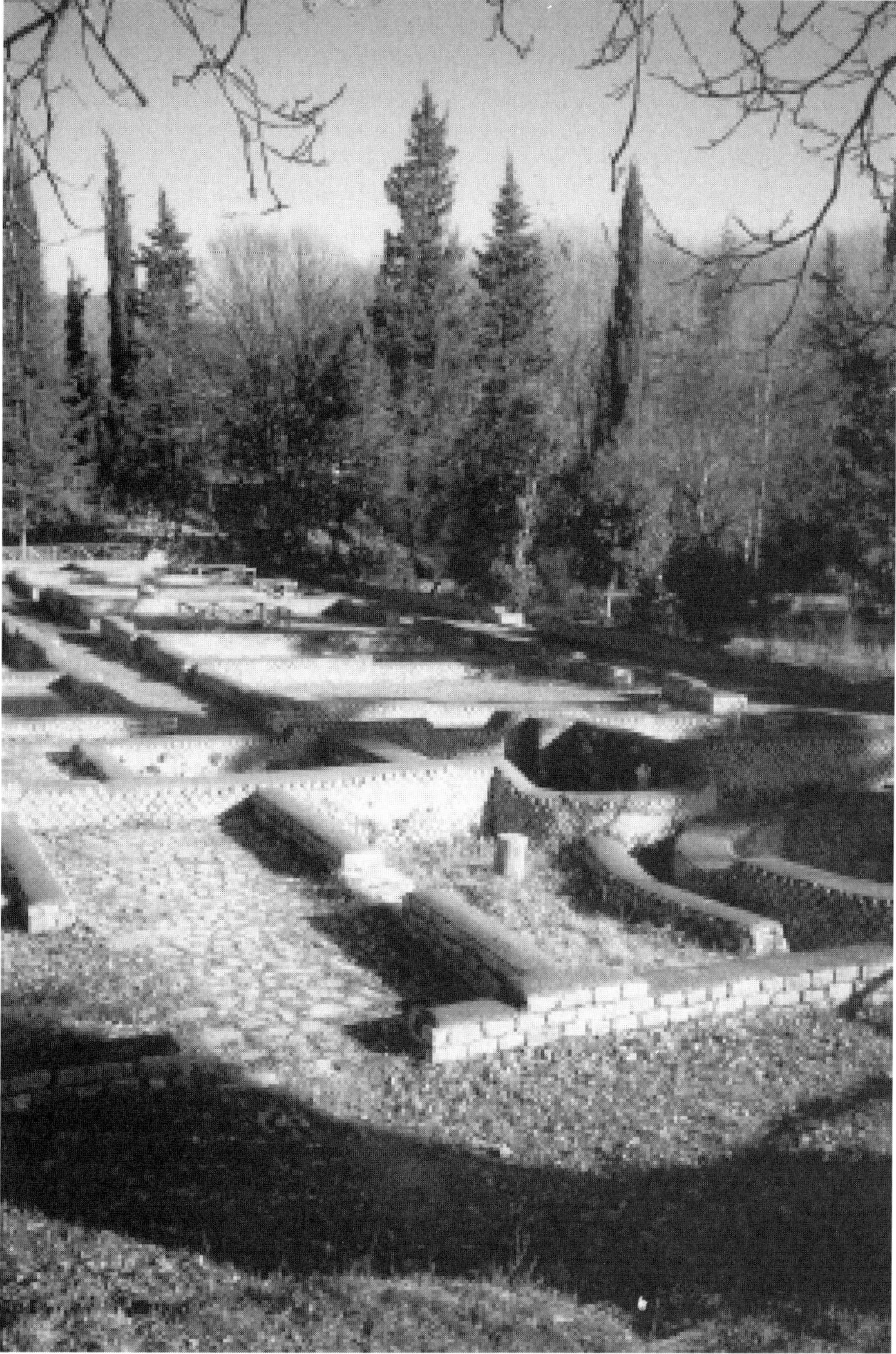

Figure 2.9 *Horace's Sabine villa. (Photo: Phil Perkins)*

Please now read extract 2.9. There will not be a detailed discussion here, but note how Horace's presentation of the city/country polarity contrasts with Virgil's.

These short pieces have enabled us to see that, already in the early empire, Rome and Italy project powerful but complex, and in some respects contradictory, images of themselves in poetry, which undoubtedly reflect the tensions in the Romans' perception of their own identity, visible, as we have seen, in other media: Italy as the hardy rustic complement to Roman imperial ambitions (extract 2.7), but in extract 2.8 the morally pure antitype against which the Romans are judged – the abandoned paradise which, it is supposed, they originally inhabited. In Horace, on the other hand, in the very different medium of the satire, the countryside is the place where the hard-pressed man of affairs might find safety, the simple life and, above all, leisure, qualities of life which the city does not provide.

We will now see how these ideas are worked out in the later and in many respects more complex presentation of Juvenal.

Juvenal – the satiric slant

You have now been introduced to the 'poetic' landscape of Italy, and its relationship not only to Rome but also to the rough, tough peasant stock which was perceived as a central part of the Roman identity. In this scenario, the empire owed its survival and success to a robust and rustic character. There was an ambiguous side to this idealized image of the Italian ancestor, for he was an aspect of Rome's 'grubby' beginnings, lending himself to ridicule within sophisticated circles and epitomizing one of the differences between town and country, not just chronologically but also culturally. You have met this sort of character above in the guise of the farmer of Virgil's *Georgics*, who rejoices in simple pleasures, presiding over a darts match and providing plain food. There is nothing but admiration for the scene in Virgil, but transferred to the medium of satire the picture of rural innocence could become one of country clownishness.

> Learn to enjoy hoeing, work and plant your allotment
> Till a hundred vegetarians could feast off its produce.
> It's quite an achievement, even out in the backwoods,
> To have made yourself the master of – well, say one lizard, even.
> (Juvenal, *Satire* 3, lines 228–31)

One interesting aspect of this poem, written about 150 years after the *Georgics*, is the landscape common to the two writers. The *ideal* of rural Italy remains the same, whether the poet takes pleasure in praising or in poking fun. How far the landscape corresponds to the ancient reality is one question you may want to keep in mind as you work through the rest of Block Two.

The satire chosen for an in-depth study is number 11, in which the poet apparently recreates uncomplicated lifestyles of the countryside but simultaneously takes the expansion of empire, and a corresponding expansion of cultural tastes, as a framework, a given of the historical period in which he lived.

You will be reading and responding to Juvenal's *Satire* 11 (extract 2.10). This poem deals in the main part with the contrast between the luxury of the imperial city and the relatively simple life of the Italian countryside. The satire should provide some helpful insights into themes raised in this block, for example the nature of cosmopolitan Rome, the economy of the countryside, the impact of empire on the capital and on the capital's Italian environment and, more conceptually, the idealization of the past to highlight the shortcomings of the present.

The second aspect to this study of the Juvenal poem will be further practice for you in peeling off the literary layers of Roman poetry. Virgil, Horace and their perceptions of Italian countryside have to be set into a context of literary traditions. Also, a subtext of sophisticated attitudes needs to be searched for. Juvenal deserves some careful attention in terms of the genre he is working with and the programmatic statements he announces at various stages in his satires. In other words, and this is a point worth reiterating, the poets and their poetry cannot be taken at face value: as 'evidence' for events and attitudes they require circumspect treatment.

Juvenal himself

We know little about this influential poet, whose work was highly thought of throughout the history of European culture. Samuel Johnson is one of a number of famous names who wrote versions of several Juvenal satires. Juvenal probably lived and wrote around the beginning of the second century AD, having survived the reign of Domitian – no easy time for anyone of independent spirit either politically or poetically. Juvenal may have been exiled to Egypt at one point, an event that would link him with Ovid and Seneca, but this remains a speculative suggestion.

The poetry

Juvenal wrote his satires in the epic metre, the dactylic hexameter. This form of verse for satire had become traditional in the literary development of Roman literature. (For instance, Horace produced several books of satire in this metre and he was following in the footsteps of the earlier satiric poet, Lucilius.) I would not like to give the impression that all writing with a satiric tone or purpose was in this epic metre. You were introduced on the audio cassette accompanying Block One to the *Apocolocyntosis*, a vicious piece of lampoonery that combined a mixture of prose and verse, a form called Menippean satire. You have also encountered extracts from the novel *Satyricon* by Petronius, a work that comically portrays a whole range of subjects from sex to social climbing. The pithy epigram could also function as satire.

'Satire' comes from the Latin *satura*, which can indicate an assortment, a hotch-potch. Roman satire not only deals with a wide variety of subject matter and allows for an equally wide variety of treatments; it also appears in different styles and forms. However, the sustained and sometimes semi-didactic diatribes about the human condition which are written in dactylic hexameter are uniquely Roman, a genre of Latin literature which it could truly call its own, without a Greek precursor.

Juvenal, then, used the dactylic hexameter form but, in spite of this being the metre of weighty or didactic material, we cannot assume that Juvenal sustains an unrelieved note of seriousness in his poetry. What he does do is to adopt an often loud and angry voice, befitting a poet who has announced (in his *Satire* 1) that *indignatio* (a fierce sense of injury or insult) *facit versum* (produces his poetry). The power of Juvenal's attacks, of suitably epic proportions, has in the past earned him a reputation of being a morally indignant poet who 'lashed the vices of the town' (that is, Rome, the capital city being presented as a distillation of corrupt manners and degraded souls). This view of Juvenal and of his poetry has been strongly challenged, particularly in the last half of the twentieth century. His character Umbricius, who leaves Rome disillusioned with and critical of city life and looks forward to the peace of the countryside (*Satire* 3), has been reassessed (among others by Braund, 1988) as himself a butt of Juvenalian irony, a self-important windbag begrudging others the vices he can no longer afford. (Even the low-cost prostitutes have priced him out of their market.) You can read part of *Satire* 3 in extract 2.11.

I would like you to bear this more recent thinking about Juvenal in mind as you work through the discussion on *Satire* 11. In some ways the demolition of long-held assumptions about Juvenal's moral purpose and motivation makes an analysis of his poems less straightforward. An earlier satirist, Persius, had declared that he had a vision of all Romans with asses' ears (*Satires* 1.121). Persius' proclamation could be a benchmark for scholars who are concerned with re-evaluating the tone and purpose of the Juvenalian satires. When Juvenal makes his uncompromising statement about a fierce sense of anger propelling his critical poetry ever onwards, can we take him seriously?

The poetic persona

'Persona' can mean 'mask': in literary criticism it is used of the speaker of a poem who is frequently distanced from, or clearly introduced as, different from the poet. The reader might experience difficulty in recognizing the distinctions, especially when sophisticated writers multiply the authoritative 'voices' within their work.

This technique, which scholars have identified but classical poets unsportingly do not spell out themselves, is the adoption of a pose which galvanizes the poetic process. This role-play begins at the outset of the work, usually in the opening declaration of intent, and consists of taking an apparently personal stand about the ideological content of the poetry. In *Satire* 3 Juvenal transforms himself into a moralistic judge, only to reveal, as the poem progresses, that this persona is one of the fictions of his poetic narrative, and fair game for the fun along with the other satirical targets; hence turning the tables on Umbricius, who seems to be a Juvenalian double, and to stand in for the satirist himself.

A useful comparison is Ovid, who in the opening two poems of his work *Amores* invents an elaborate scenario in which the love god, *Amor*, or more familiarly Cupid, shoots the unfortunate poet, thereby forcing him to fall in love and automatically write love poetry. The actions of Cupid are described with a good deal of humorous poetic panache as Ovid berates the god with mock despair. He accuses Cupid of hijacking the role of divine inspirer from the proper god of the Arts, Apollo, and of defying job demarcation. Cupid is blamed for the fact that each time Ovid steels himself to produce an epic or a tragedy he finds himself slipping into the poetic metres and topics of more frivolous genres.

For this reason many critics feel that Ovid's love poems are only in the most marginal sense 'autobiographical'. Ovid has decided to role-play the lover in order to write love poetry. There is certainly a view that Juvenal made a comparably melodramatic gesture, raising himself up to the heights of righteous indignation in order to write satiric poetry. The very loftiness of the word *indignatio*, passionate exasperation, sounds rather like one of the abstract deities the Romans were likely to produce a temple and a set of rituals for!

When you engaged with the poetry of Virgil, Horace and Propertius in Block One you were required to juggle various factors: their individual experiences in the late republic and early principate, the literary legacies they inherited in their chosen genres and their distinct ways of either 'buying into' or remaining relatively detached from the political situation of their time. It would seem that the task with poetry like Juvenal's is an equally sophisticated one.

Satire 11

The structure of the poem is clearly demarcated. A long introduction exemplifies the theme of living beyond one's means. Then a 'dear friend' is addressed, named in the Latin text as Persicus. The name suggests a fictitious proponent of Persian luxury. Persicus is invited to a modest dinner which demonstrates how plentiful and satisfying simple fare can be. The guest is to expect plain food, plain furniture and local, unsophisticated slaves. There will be no exotic and fancy entertainment. This 'taste' of the country is held up as a retreat from the tedium of the town, although this 'tedium' is really the narrator's subjective and world-weary view of the 'excitements' Rome had to offer.

Exercise

Read through the poem (extract 2.10) once so that you can follow the shape of the narrative we have outlined. Perhaps you will have an initial reaction to the pose the poet is adopting. After this first reading (it is up to you whether you also read all the footnotes at this stage) you should return to the discussion and more detailed questions below.

Discussion

You may already have detected a tongue-in-cheek tone to some of this celebration of the frugal life. We thought that the rural dinner sounded fairly spectacular in range and delicacies and that the food, like the poem itself, with its mythical and historical allusions, was concocted for an educated palate! We would not want to prejudice your response at this early stage, but if you did perceive an undercurrent of irony, especially in the comic picture of the 'closet' consumer of conspicuous luxury, be assured that the discussion will take this into account in the summary and overview of the whole satire.

Exercise

Now reread the first fifty-five lines, the literary hors d'oeuvres to the rustic banquet, and respond to the questions below. And do make use of the notes this time.

1. Can you detect a consistent 'sermon'? What lesson is Juvenal driving home?
2. What range of examples does Juvenal produce to strengthen his arguments? Look at contemporary (such as lines 1–22), legendary (such as lines 32–3), specific and general categories.

3 What does this introduction tell the modern reader about behaviour in Roman society in Juvenal's day?

4 Do the poet's tone and his treatment of his subject suggest a clear and uncompromising attitude which he wishes his audience to adopt? (More simply, can you detect any double messages here?)

Discussion

1 *Satire* 11 is regarded as a less aggressive piece of writing than some of Juvenal's earlier poems and a good example of Juvenal's 'mellowing out' in his response to Roman vices. (The diminishing of his *indignatio* is discussed in Braund, 1988.) The satirist certainly goes on to suggest positive steps one can take to avoid the cares and pressures of a life of ostentation, the 'spend, spend, spend' of a society where not just wealth but the display of wealth counted for so much. All the same, the picture of extravagance and degradation which the poet paints for the reader packs quite a punch, and this is a typically Juvenalian grand slam attack on the human examples he has chosen to illustrate his point. What he seems to be saying in this first section is that there is a tragic as well as a comic side to those who live beyond their means and have lost all sense of proportion and priorities in satisfying their appetites. Those caught up in the desire to dine well do so whatever the consequences for their social status and for the state of the family finances. Many (but note not all) of his human examples come to grief. The suicide of the bankrupt gourmet Apicius is mentioned, as is the nobleman Rutilus, who will probably resort to selling himself into the gladiator school when all the money has run out.

2 You will have gathered from the commentary that we cannot be sure about the identity of every character whom Juvenal introduces (for example notes 1 and 9). The addressee of the first line is probably Tiberius Claudius Atticus, who discovered a treasure at the end of the first century AD and passed on the fortune to his enterprising son. This son you will be meeting in a Block Three, as he was an important benefactor of Greek cities. Apicius – a sort of Mrs Beeton of his day (his cookbook is still available in paperback) – has survived the centuries, but Rutilus is not known to the modern reader. We can only presume that some of the names had become bywords for the weaknesses Juvenal wishes to portray. Intriguingly, in his very first satire,

when the poet announces why and how he is going to produce his critique of society, he states that it is safest to attack the dead, rather a reversal of *de mortuis nil nisi bonum* (those we speak no ill of, literally '[speak] nothing but good of the dead'). Frequently in Juvenal's poetry historical figures are used as negative role models and seem to be supplementing mythical exemplars so popular with other poets when they wished to make a point.

You would have noticed the reference to Ulysses, who won the armour of Achilles (lines 32–3). The shield of Achilles was mentioned in the section on Actium in Block One. Ovid, in his epic poem *Metamorphoses*, described the competition between the wily and persuasive Ulysses and the man of action, Ajax. Juvenal quite cavalierly juxtaposes this legendary scene with the quick sketches he has made about choosing a wife or gaining a seat in the senate. The question the poet poses is, 'Are you man enough for the job, or is the wife, the career or the heroic fighting ability out of your league?' All these illustrations are predicated on the pronouncement of the Delphic oracle about knowing yourself and your limitations. This seems to be the key text of the 'sermon'.

The armour Ulysses won was not ultimately a comfortable fit. Juvenal then turns back to address some fictitious contemporary and reiterate the madness of living life with an endless open mouth. The needs of his belly swallow up all his income and the family capital as well. (It is possible that the reader is supposed to keep Ulysses in mind at this point, because he endangered himself and his crew in the search for plunder and gifts of guest friendship. He also frequently cursed the dictates of his stomach as a necessary part of the mortal condition.)

Those who manage to flee their creditors and keep *la dolce vita* at Baiae (a notorious seaside resort for the dissolute), a very congenial self-imposed exile, still miss the capital city, the entertainment of the circus and the amphitheatre. Both were venues where 'high society' could be seen and could flaunt its wealth alongside the displays in the arena and the chariot ring.

3 Using satirical comment to reconstruct social realities can be a risky business, but there are conclusions to be drawn about some customs and practices, and certainly about attitudes and values which you have already encountered in this block and in Block One. What strikes one initially is the very public and open-air life Juvenal is describing in the city. All the regular meeting places – the baths, the arcades and the theatre foyers – are buzzing with

the latest scandal. 'What gets a bigger horse-laugh ... than a gourmand gone broke?' (lines 2–3). The mention of the market, where few could escape prowling creditors, comes a few lines later. It is also the place where the delicacies are on show, the very temptations that have reduced the gluttons to this sorry state of affairs. A more sophisticated and prevalent image of exposure is that of Rome's being a 'see-through' society. The man who cannot afford the lifestyle he is desperate to maintain is like a derelict house. No one can fail to notice the cracks. Nor can any of the more nefarious actions be kept a secret – hocking the family plate or pledging Mummy's portrait. All this seems to be taking place in the public domain. The worst-case scenario is the loss of the ring which denoted the position of an *eques* (line 45) (see Essay Five).

The trail of losses and disasters Juvenal outlines – and he is very skilled at relentless expansion and detail of this kind (the literary term for this device is amplification) – demonstrates the rapid decline in social status a reputable member of the wealthy classes could experience once they were caught up in the whirlwind parties. These binges of eating and drinking and trying out all the delicacies, which were a feature of the expanded empire of Juvenal's day, had other aspects to them. There was a great deal on offer from all corners of the globe and foreign imports were not confined to food. Rome, as the metropolis, offered maximum choice. A little further on in the discussion you will be looking at the kind of exotica an extravagant host might provide as part of the over-dinner entertainment.

4 You might have been alerted to some equivocation quite early on in this introduction. In spite of the poet's protestations about behaving sensibly and reasonably, cutting your coat according to your cloth you might say, he drives home the point about luxury being acceptable if you can afford it. The condemnation is for those who are unable to recognize the true state of their financial affairs or who wilfully ignore their lack of means. For Juvenal's readers, knowing (as they presumably would have done) that Atticus had made a lucky find, the message is a cynical one. The rich are not always deserving and fortune is indiscriminate in handing out the breaks. Elsewhere, and particularly in *Satire* 3 (extract 2.11), Juvenal wrily, even grimly, observes that poverty has a social stigma, whether one brings it on oneself or not.

Juvenal's world is not a fair one, and this fact helps to create the ideal circumstances for the satirist. Juvenal shows contempt for those who behave inappropriately for their station, crossing boundaries of social class and masquerading as their superiors or, in some cases, as their inferiors (Reekmans, 1971, pp.154–61). This distorts the proper hierarchy of relations and cries out for satirical comment, because it truly is a topsy-turvy world. For Juvenal this is the very stuff of satire. Juvenal harps on about the licence enjoyed by the wealthy gourmand and exaggerates the failings of the impoverished to comical effect (Weisinger, 1972, pp.229–30). The introduction of 'know thyself' (line 29) undercuts the 'moral' further because it is a philosophical cliché skittishly applied to those who are ignorant of their bank balance. As the poem progresses it becomes clearer that Juvenal is actually quite aware of his own anomalous position, posing as a social critic but forced to live and compromise in a degenerate society. Juvenal does – and with a sense of self-irony – 'know himself'.

To a certain extent this observation links into discussions about the poetic persona. Is this genial and upright host – the 'I' of *Satire* 11 – not necessarily the poet himself but a target of the poet? In a way this is not a vital question and it is really unresolvable. The important thing is that you feel you can highlight places where the poet's stance is in itself a consciously hypocritical one and to work out whether he is drawing attention to double standards or self-delusion.

Exercise

Now read the description of the dinner (again with the notes as your guide) and respond to the following questions. Read as far as line 115.

1. Why does Juvenal introduce the figures of Evander, Hercules and Aeneas before he tells Persicus the menu?
2. What picture of the countryside, its activities and its inhabitants is implied in the itemization of the food?
3. How does the meal contrast with the 'prodigality' of the town but also with the frugality of the distant and rural past?
4. What were the main features of this past? (Look closely at the relationship between the country and the city, and the assumptions about how the Roman character was formed. Thinking back to the section on the Italian poets might be helpful at this point.)

Discussion

1 Juvenal promises Persicus that he is not preaching one thing and practising another. He really can live and eat simply. The comparison with Evander entertaining the great Hercules or the Trojan hero Aeneas is a neat little bit of legendary aside which appears very apt. Evander is the archetypically 'good' host. The allusion to Evander is an encouragement to the guest not to disdain the basic hospitality Juvenal is able to offer. On the one hand it gives the invitation, the host and the guest a comical sense of importance. From another viewpoint, this is Juvenal playing a tantalizing game and dashing the hopes of a decent meal. Paradoxically, expectations are raised again, almost immediately, as Juvenal outlines the menu.

2 Fresh produce, freshly picked – the image of the bailiff's wife is a cosy and protective one, a nice touch of rural charm – and nothing comes from the market: all this sounds like a hymn to self-sufficiency and certainly an ecologically sound meal (Jones, 1990, pp.162–3, reproduced in offprint 2.2). Perhaps you feel that this is going over the top here and being a little bit anachronistic in the characterization of the passage, but there is a definite feeling of a Golden Age existence in this description. Juvenal does not have to make any effort in the preparations; his estate and his slaves provide everything and the result is an array of wholesome food. You will notice that a Syrian variety of pear appears in the fruit basket. These were transplanted to Tarentum in Italy and are a hint of the altered crop landscape as well as the early 'fruits' of the empire. You might like to contrast this with the first *Georgics* extract (extract 2.7), where Virgil promotes the produce of Italy over the tasty foreign imports.

3 Juvenal freely admits that this is a luxurious dinner in comparison with what was on offer in the old days. Actually the menu is inspired by a poem by Martial, a contemporary and friend of Juvenal, and not entirely dreamed up by Juvenal. It is quite possible that both poets were working from a mythical model – the ideal rustic meal. The poet reminds the reader how rarely meat would have appeared at the table in earlier and harder times. Juvenal's dinner is taking place in a festival season, so there is some excuse for extravagance of this kind. Even so, the point is valid: animals were slaughtered on special occasions as sacrifices to the gods and only then should one enjoy the eating of meat. (You might be reminded of Horace and his

suggestion that abstention from good wine was appropriate until the permanent removal of Cleopatra could be celebrated with due thanksgiving to Olympus.)

Weisinger (1972, p.235) sums up the whole scenario very neatly: the Romans of earlier times were so far from *luxuria* that the modest meal the poet has just proposed would have been considered a banquet in those days. Here, the middle position adopted by the poet is clear: he stands somewhere between the austere frugality of the ancients and the monstrous prodigality of his contemporaries.

What did you make of the historical figures who were trotted out? (I use this verb deliberately; this was a familiar array for Latin poetry and prose when the writer wanted to make a point about the sterner stock of early Roman leaders. Their names also appear in *Satires* 2 and 8.) Juvenal only needs to refer to these characters in a kind of shorthand because they came equipped with the famous anecdotes about their frugality and discipline, for instance Curius and his roast turnip, Cato the martinet in all things and the two censors who vied with each other in producing anti-luxury laws. Hence, Weisinger sees Juvenal's picture of rustic virtue as 'almost a parody of austerity'.

4 The rustic scene is rounded off with another contrast, with the crude designs of the couches, the country children, an integrated communal existence set against the present-day Romans' pathetic preoccupations with elaborate furniture. (Naming his contemporaries as descendants of the Trojan stock conveys a double message, as the Trojan prince Aeneas was believed to have fought to establish the original Roman territory, a positive model which his heirs have failed to follow (see Block One on Actium). Alternatively, the lovers of luxury are keeping up another tradition associated with the Trojans, that of foreign effeteness.)

The emphasis on fancy tastes for *objets d'art* is a sharp reminder of present realities in Juvenal's time. The translation we are using in extract 2.10 refers to 'republican troops' throughout this section, but the original Latin focuses on a single 'typical' soldier of bygone days, which gives a more vivid and intimate picture altogether. The portrayal of the rough soldier (the adjective used in the original, *rudis*, can mean without aesthetic sense as well as rough physically) and his attitude to the arts of Greece seem particularly whimsical at this point. The republican soldier recycles the artefacts of colonized territories to blazon specifically Roman images on his armour. And is there an added irony here if we recall the actions of the glutton breaking up the silver plate in the introduction to the poem?

Felton and Lee (1972) view this scene differently. They see the rough soldier as a positive role model with no sarcastic subtext: 'It is noteworthy that in line 100 Juvenal uses words with derogatory overtones, *rudis, nescius,* to express not disapproval but commendation. The use of *rudis* in line 143 and of *incultus* [uncultured] in line 146 is similar.'

In a final image we see this helmet cruelly displayed above an enemy of Rome who is about to die at the soldier's hand. The rustic soldier has become more of an example of cruel barbarism than a symbol of older moral values (Weisinger, 1972, p.237).

The soldier image gives a satisfying circular feel to this whole topic, since the consuls and dictators of old who had set up the train of thought were also active military men, specifically commanders in the field. The implication is a shared experience, a bonding between leaders and rank and file which had made the Roman army great. As ever, there is a subtext to this message as well. The ostentation of the soldier's helmet marks up the fighting spirit of Rome, the very lust to conquer which has resulted in the availability of luxury items from around the world. So you should be able to see the nature of the conundrum Juvenal is deliberately highlighting. His moral perspective seems to shift and to take the reader along with him. His concluding comment to this section concerning envy – 'if you're jealous by nature' – if you are the envious type – is disingenuous to say the least. It is part of his teasing technique to assume that Persicus would find this set-up – the prospect of eating porridge out of earthenware pots – appealing.

Exercise

We indicated at the start of section 3.3 that the literary Romans struck a whole set of attitudes to the rustic past and the military prowess it had supposedly nurtured. As you read the next section of *Satire* 11, look out for further familiar issues dealing with the simple pleasures of the past and the present craving for excessive luxury. Does Juvenal suggest a resolution to the dilemma?

Now read to line 159.

Discussion

We are just going to make a few points here because we have already established the groundwork for some possible approaches to this poem both as a source for factual evidence and a useful barometer for attitudes and ambivalences about empire.

The gods have been encountered before, in so far as Juvenal has alluded to sacrifice to them. He expands on this with his reference to the primitive clay image of Jupiter and his connection of this to the simpler, more straightforward relationship Romans had with their gods in the past. Protection was guaranteed for these Romans and the capital was saved from barbarian invasion. The emphasis on the indigenous materials for statues and tables (all 'home-grown') makes the jaded palate of the modern millionaire even more worthy of condemnation. Now it is suggested that he cannot enjoy food unless his table is ridiculously ornate. The list of trappings gives a real sense of what luxury items the breadth and expanse of empire could provide. It simultaneously implies that Roman tastes have been colonized by territories in or close to its ambit of power. In other words, several topics have been revisited and the same points driven home.

Juvenal finally returns to the description of his proposed dinner, and this time he indicates what his guest should *not* expect: none of the fancy furniture or cutlery which is so important to and bound up with the status of the rich, who feel obliged to 'pay and display' (compare Figure 2.10). You might find it interesting to compare Juvenal's humorous vignette on elaborate carving and culinary flourishes with scenes from Trimalchio's feast, a character whom you have already met in this block (and will meet again in Essay Four). Trimalchio, Petronius' self-made millionaire, puts on all manner of vulgar displays. The dishes are part of the entertainment and many of them are styled into such weird and wonderful shapes as to cease to resemble food in any way; rather, they become part of the 'architecture' of the table.

Juvenal expresses relief that his young and local servants are equally unskilled in carving and thieving. The scene becomes a metaphor of innocence and corruption. Weisinger (1972, p.239) points out that the uncouth lad has experienced life in a similar fashion to the young goat which is to be the main course. You may want to refer back to those lines (68–70). All these servants are as 'home-grown' and as wholesome as the food and wine they serve. *Rudis* is also used to describe the young serving boy, linking him to the ignorant soldier. Both are rough round the edges. It is quite easy to construct by

Figure 2.10 *Wall painting from the tomb of the magistrate Vestorius Priscus depicting silverware, Pompeii. Museo Nazionale Archeologico, Naples.*

contrast the figure of the imported slave, knowing, sophisticated and alien to the pure air and countryside of Italy. However, Weisinger does point out that the servants, like the banquet, are not really replicas of the old moral human stock. They do steal but not very efficiently; they too are in the halfway house between past innocence and present urbanity.

Exercise

Please finish reading the poem and see if you can tie up its conclusion with the main points the poet has made along the way.

Decide for yourself how successful the poet has been in his persuasion. Pay particular attention to his promise that Persicus will escape the stresses and strains of urban life, at least temporarily. Do you feel that Juvenal 'hedges his bets' at the end?

Discussion

In the final section Juvenal continues to itemize the exotic aspects of a Roman banquet which Persicus is to be deprived of. This is a continuation of the comedy, as the poet does make rather a meal of the absence of sexy Spanish dancers and encourages his guest to feel disappointed that they will not be there after all. He paints a lurid picture of the nasty habits and antisocial behaviour one might find at a rich man's banquet and gives further examples of what is allowable: 'The rich are forgiven such conduct'. This is a reprise of the theme in the opening of the poem. Somehow wealth expands the boundaries of what is acceptable and appropriate behaviour. Juvenal highlights the hypocrisy once again.

Juvenal is continuing in his teasing and tantalizing technique by itemizing the entertainments he will not provide. All the same, there is a serious note in this last section. The poet does reiterate the point that wealth lends legitimacy to the most indecorous behaviour. The foreign habits that Rome has picked up will have no place in Juvenal's establishment. He is still able and willing to provide the epic poetry of Virgil to enhance the ambience of his evening. Cheap and sensationalist distractions are not his idea of relaxation. Weisinger believes that Juvenal is twisting the knife with Persicus by reminding him of his cares just as he appears to be offering him a respite from them. The message seems to be 'take a break from the rat-race, the bustle and pressures of Rome, and relax on my country estate', but 'this catalogue of cares is prompted by the same kind of ironic humor which prompted the lengthy description of the Spanish dancers who will not be present' (Weisinger, 1972, p.240).

Weisinger concludes that Juvenal is in essence a realist. The present cannot be escaped, and the final twist to the poet's argument is possibly the most effective, given that his addressee is a character who is not likely to be easily convinced. The argument ends rather unexpectedly, along the lines of 'all things in moderation'. ('Keep to the golden mean' was a wise saw of the ancient world rather akin to the 'know thyself' which you met earlier.) The sophisticated pleasures can be heightened as long as they are not over-indulged. Juvenal provides an alternative to city pleasures but does not seriously advocate relinquishing the life he and his guest have been born to. Think back to the discussion on Umbricius and the poetic persona. In

Satire 3 the person speaking, Umbricius, is leaving for the country but not Juvenal himself, who is the addressee.

The last lines of *Satire* 11 reveal that this rustic meal has all along been taking place in *Rome,* within earshot of the circus. This forces us as readers to reappraise the poem's town/country contrast. Elsewhere in the literature, Pliny's *Letters* for instance or in the poems of Statius, we hear of villas that were essentially sophisticated urban enclaves (with all 'mod cons') in the countryside. Juvenal has cleverly recreated a simple rustic scenario in the heart of the metropolis.

Juvenal's final retreat from the moral high ground has been signposted throughout this poem. The poet indicates to us, the readers, that some sort of compromise is accepted and desirable. Juvenal has certainly not opted out of the society he satirizes. We have a poem by Martial (*Epigrams* 12.18) in which he visualizes his friend Juvenal doing a weary round of the wealthy houses in Rome (paying his respects):

> The attitude of resignation and pessimism characteristic of *Satire* 11 is possible only in a poet who has seen that the course of history is inevitable and wishes to withdraw himself from that progress rather than to rage at it. The invitation is not merely to dinner, it is an invitation to join the poet in escaping from this historical process for a short while.
> (Weisinger, 1972, p.240)

Conclusion

Juvenal's *Satire* 11 is a witty and incisive attack on what imperial Rome has become. At the same time it is a not entirely serious reworking of clichés about an idealized past and of literary conventions, conventions that articulated and perpetuated beliefs concerning the characters and characteristics of Rome's progress from rustic survival to its cosmopolitan and corrupted present. The poem does convey to the student of Roman history a number of features of life in the country and the city. The testimony is not necessarily direct and sometimes the use of other evidence – literary and archaeological – has to be brought into play before we can reach any firm conclusions.

One of the skills you will have been developing throughout this block is integrating the range of evidence focused on in each section. Many of the issues raised by analysing aspects of the Juvenal satire are explored elsewhere in the block: the importance of status, the consumer economy, the retreat offered by the Italian countryside where something of the legendary Italian character could be retrieved, and so on. The aim of this section, the study of a satiric poem, was to assist you in teasing out significant attitudes towards empire and how it was perceived by the educated commentators of the time. Juvenal seems to be aware of, yet still sentimental about, the idealization of country life in Italy. Satire caricatures social life but it also reveals concerns and truths about Roman identity – an identity that was more fluid than fixed, especially as its culture expanded along with its power throughout the known world.

3.4 Economic aspects of the relationship between Rome and Italy

The landscape of Italy served as an inspiration for the Roman poets, but the image they present is invariably romanticized. The poetic constructs of Virgil, Horace and Juvenal were not intended to present an image of rural life as it was. For the large majority of people living in the country, life would have been hard. Many would have lived at a subsistence level, and many would have had servile status. In this section we will consider the countryside of Italy and beyond as a setting for economic activity. In the first part of this section we will concentrate on this tougher 'real world' by looking at some further economic activities in Italy. You have already started studying the economy in Pompeii in section 2.4 and here you will continue by first looking at rural Italy and then going on to consider some aspects of the economic relationships between Italy, Rome and the wider empire. In the second part of this section you will focus on a specific part of the economy of Italy: wine production in the country and its consumption in Rome. In this section you will need to use *Experiencing Rome* and the Offprints Book (for further texts see extracts 2.12 and 2.13 in the Supplementary Texts and the discussion in offprint 2.1).

Rome, Italy and the economy

Exercise

The first activity is to read Essay Seven in *Experiencing Rome*, 'Power, culture and identity in the Roman economy'. The essay covers a wide range of topics but in this section of Block Two the focus is on the relationship between Rome and Italy. The essay covers six main topics:

1 a comparison between literary descriptions of estate management and the realities as excavated in a Roman villa in Tuscany;

2 the bureaucratic management of imperial sheep flocks;

3 imperial involvement in economic management;

4 the empire-wide organization and management of trade in foodstuffs between the provinces and Rome via Ostia;

5 how an Italian or Roman identity might be expressed in the choice of articles purchased and used by individuals;

6 finally, how economic activity can be used to define and represent an identity.

As you finish reading each of these six topics in the essay, note down whether you think each topic relates to the following block themes, and briefly give your reasons:

(a) the relationship between the city and the country (idealized or otherwise);

(b) the relationship between Rome and Italy;

(c) the relationship between emperor and subject;

(d) social status and identity.

Discussion

The discussion is arranged by topics and treats each question in turn.

1 (a) The discussion of the villa at Settefinestre closely concerns the relationship between city and country. A rural villa was chosen for discussion here as a contrast to the cities of Rome, Pompeii and Ostia which you have previously studied. The villa, with its solid, decorated walls and ordered ground plan, can be seen as a projection of city living into the countryside. The ownership of the rural land by an urban élite can be viewed in a similar way and the productive capacity of the countryside can be seen as being siphoned off to fuel the luxurious lifestyle of the élite of city dwellers. Conversely, the creation of 'civilized' rural estates can be seen as a projection of urban *luxuria* into the countryside. On a slightly different tack, perhaps we can also see the vineyards within the city walls of Pompeii as a projection of a rural (possibly an idyllic) lifestyle into the city.

(b) The villa can also be seen as an example of the relationship between a part of Italy and Rome. The area around Settefinestre is not typical of the whole of Italy and so it is not safe to assume that all of Italy was similar. None the less, the notion of the countryside as a productive area also suitable for leisure and investment echoes some of the poetic images studied in the previous section.

(c) The relationship between emperor and subject is not actually addressed; instead the villa embodies the relationship between master and slave. However, this might parallel the relationship between the emperor and his subjects. The two relationships might even converge in cases where the estate was imperially owned and the emperor would actually be the master, although it is likely that the emperor would have acted through intermediaries.

(d) Social status and identity are not directly addressed either, but the villa does provide evidence for the material conditions of both slaves and élite slaveowners.

2 (a) In the case of the sheep there is a nice tension between the city officials who are harassing the presumably innocent rural shepherds. Here we see an attempt by the city authorities to exercise their legal jurisdiction over inhabitants of the countryside.

(b) The events at Bovianum are further evidence of the kinds of activities that went on in Italy and can be contrasted with life in Rome.

(c) The episode clearly illustrates imperial power being brought to bear on the city officials by the imperial administrators. The relationship between the emperor and the magistrates seems to be based on fear of investigation and punishment, whereas the relationship between the shepherds and the emperor is more like paternal protection.

(d) The inscription details the relationships between a variety of individuals with different social status. The magistrates attempt to exert their authority over the humble shepherds and imperial freedmen and defy imperial power. In opposition to this we see a chain of hierarchical status which runs from the imperial freedmen to the praetorian prefects who derive their status from the emperor. We learn little of their individual identities, but their identities are defined with reference to one another and to their legal or political authority.

3 Dealing with all four issues together, the involvement of the emperor in economic affairs can be seen as ordering and regulating relationships between city and country as well as between Rome and Italy. This might be indirect, through the emperor's role as supreme magistrate, or direct intervention. The emperor acted either for his own financial benefit or to enhance his own prestige and imperial identity by attempting to

manage the economy in ways beneficial to the people of Rome and citizens in the provinces.

4 (a) The organization of the supply of foodstuffs to the city of Rome can be seen as a magnification of the usual relationship between a city and the surrounding countryside, where the produce of the countryside supplies the market and feeds the people of the city. Here the provinces of the empire can be seen fulfilling the same role and supplying the city of Rome with the produce it required.

(b) No doubt much of the produce of Italy went to feed the mouths of Romans, but Italy had a special relationship with Rome. Italy was exempt from taxes and produce was not requisitioned in Italy. Therefore the economy in Italy was less centrally managed than in some other provinces.

(c) As in issue 3, the efficient imperial administration of food supply to Rome and the army is a tangible example of the emperor maintaining the well-being of the imperial subjects, even if others had to suffer taxes or appropriations to supply the resources which the emperor could then pass on.

(d) Social status and identity are not really addressed, but in Rome beneficiaries of the *annona* did have to be citizens in order to receive the food dole.

5 The example discussed, of Italian tableware, only really addresses issues (b) and (d), although other examples might illustrate other issues. The tableware first made in Italy spread through the peninsula and became common in the city of Rome. It became associated with the spread of Roman and Italian culture through the empire as it was used by conquering armies and as provincial areas were drawn into the Roman economy. As discussed in the essay, the use of Roman material culture can also be seen as an expression of Roman identity.

6 The use of representations of economic activities on tombstones only directly relates to (d) because the trade or profession of individuals is being used to help define the identity and role of the deceased.

In this exercise you have seen how the economy can be linked to the themes of the block and more generally the course too. In the next part of this section you will investigate a relationship between Rome and one part of the Italian economy in more detail.

Wine, power and culture

In this section you will investigate another aspect of the relationship between Rome and Italy. During the early empire senators were required to own land in Italy in order to qualify for the title and status. In Essay Seven you studied a landed estate with its villa at Settefinestre. There the estate produced wine which generated wealth for the landowner, presumably a senator. The fertile areas of Italy, particularly those close to Rome, were peppered with similar villas and estates, although none have been excavated to the same degree as Settefinestre. Altogether these estates represent a substantial capacity for agricultural production and large-scale investment in land.

Exercise

We now want you to read an article in the Offprints Book, 'Wine and wealth in ancient Italy' by Nicholas Purcell. This ties together senatorial wealth, land ownership and wine production and uses them to link the countryside of Italy to the city of Rome.

Although the article is only nineteen pages long it contains a lot of ideas and information. We suggest you ignore the footnotes if you prefer to and just read the main text; the footnotes refer mainly to other publications and ancient sources which provide support for Purcell's ideas. The author also uses many Latin words and expressions along with specialist terms; these are listed and translated after the article in the Offprints Book. Some of the Latin terms are essential to the text and there is no common or easy English translation; others are part of Purcell's personal style of scholarly writing.

Now read offprint 2.3. As you read, think about and make notes on the themes of *luxuria*, rural Italy and the relationship between Rome and Italy.

Discussion

Purcell takes on several of the themes of this block. He starts with the history of vine-growing in Italy, beginning by stating that he believes that economic history must be understood in conjunction with the social and cultural history of the period. This is a methodological statement. Purcell believes that it is necessary to study the history of different aspects of past societies all together in order to understand them better. He also believes that forms of evidence derived from ancient writings and those derived from modern archaeology should be used together to develop a deeper understanding (this is not made clear in Purcell's introduction, but it emerges as the article develops),

Figure 2.11 *Reconstruction of a hand-powered wine press. Museo della Civiltà Romana, Rome. (Photo: Phil Perkins)*

although he does say that the orthodoxy is based on a 'traditional and limited selection of evidence'. Purcell advocates a broad approach to the subject, and even considers the usefulness of evidence which derives not from the classical world but from the more recent history of France. He also considers the role of wine in society.

In section II attitudes to vines are considered, largely from the viewpoint of the Roman élite, and the idea of *luxuria* is particularly relevant to this section. Purcell concludes the section by suggesting that vineyards were an indulgence and that Roman senators were not closely involved in growing vines (pp.40–1). In section III the evidence for vineyards in Italy during the late republic is summarized and the section ends by seeing the time of Augustus as an important period of change. Although mainly about the republican period, it does set the scene for the changes to come, and also quotes several pieces of evidence from the imperial period.

Purcell introduces the archaeological evidence for a crisis in Italian wine production in the first century AD in section IV and contrasts it with literary sources (Pliny the Younger) which are contradictory. The 'crisis' theory suggests that Italian producers could not compete with new production areas in Spain and southern France, and Purcell effectively criticizes this theory. He also suggests that there is more evidence for élite involvement in wine production in this period in Italy. In section V the emphasis is shifted from trade in wine to its production and consumption, and it is suggested that wine consumption can be related to the social and cultural phenomenon of urbanization. In section VI Purcell attempts to draw together his various themes to produce an outline of the history of vine-growing in Italy. He draws a contrast between fine wines with a limited production and mass-produced, low-cost wines. The suggestion is that the supposed crisis in Italian wine production is really a shift from producing small quantities of fine wine to producing large quantities of cheap wine for the ever-thirsty and growing population of the city of Rome. Purcell ends by suggesting that this supposed crisis is a figment of the scholarly mind caused by a lack of understanding of how the wine market works, and that far from being in crisis the early empire was a period when the Italian wine trade was booming.

Overall, Purcell gathers together a large quantity of quite diverse arguments and develops a strong case for his point of view. As well as overturning a previous theory about what happened in Italian wine production he also sketches out a dynamic relationship between Rome and Italy that is fundamentally economic in nature, and because of the changing attitudes of the élite landowners to wine

> production it also has implications for power and wealth in Italy. If we accept Purcell's new hypothesis that the first century AD was a boom time in wine production and that the élite were interested in producing wine for sale in Rome, we can then extend the analysis by suggesting that the land-owning élite generated a portion of their wealth by producing wine in the countryside of Italy for sale in the city of Rome. This leads to the possibility that part of the status and power of the Roman élite derived from the produce of Italy and to some extent the position and power of the élite were maintained by selling intoxicating wine to the Roman populace. At this point perhaps we are beginning to strain our evidence and pile up too many hypotheses, but it does provide a stimulus to investigate new areas and consider questions of whether any form of social control was practised by the Roman élite, and if so whether the mechanisms of control were intentional or coincidental.

In this section you have seen that Rome and Italy were intricately linked throughout a range of economic activities. These links extend from very general issues of imperial policy down to the details of wine-making. You have also studied how the economy can be related to the themes of other sections in the block, such as Romanization, cities and the poetic imagination. Some of the connections might have seemed tenuous or you may not have been convinced of their importance, but the underlying point of this section is that the economy needs to be studied in the context of all the other political, military, cultural and social history that goes with it, and that a great diversity of sources of evidence can be drawn from the Roman world to help understand the ancient economy.

Conclusion to Block Two: Roman or Italian?

Italy represented Rome's first expansion and conquest. In many ways Italy was a Roman invention and the term *Italia* masks the diversity inherent in the peninsula both before and after the Social War. Nevertheless Italy was united, first by opposing Rome and then by Rome's grant of citizenship. It was Rome that fostered a sense of unity for Italy by promoting a shared identity through aspects such as similar architectural features, amenities and administration, even if many of these things were not all strictly Roman in origin. Italy was Romanized and often the distinctions between Rome and Italy become hard to identify and sustain. Often Rome meant Italy and Italy meant Rome. After all, following the Social War the Italians were citizens of Rome and contributed substantially to the political, military and artistic life that can be broadly labelled as 'Roman'.

This uniting of things Italian and Roman can be seen in the impact that the empire had on the Italian peninsula. Wealth and prestige were derived from Italian land and its productivity was influenced by the acquisition of imperial territory. However, to say that there was a seamless merging of Roman and Italian identities is less convincing. The towns of Italy did not look exactly alike and a sense of local tradition and identity could be maintained. It is difficult to reconstruct attitudes to Rome and the degree and rate at which people regarded themselves as Roman or retained a sense of local identity. The élite may have firmly aligned themselves with Rome while the perspective of the urban poor may have been very different. A sense of this different attitude to what it was to be Roman is captured in the literature that emphasizes the difference between the corruption of Rome and the simplicity of the Italian countryside. Here the merging of the Roman and Italian identity is challenged. This may often represent a rhetorical, a moral and sometimes an ironic debate which deliberately polarizes lifestyles, but it may have been underpinned by an element of truth. It is not difficult to imagine that for the Italian rural peasantry Rome was distant and distinct; labels such as 'Roman' and 'Italian' may have had some meaning, but on a daily basis power and identity may have been constructed and negotiated by other means.

It is also possible to question the continuity of the special relationship between Rome and Italy. In the early years of the empire Italy continued to provide the army, supply senators and be regarded as the homeland. But with the consolidation of the empire and the expansion of citizenship from the latter part of the first century AD, the primacy of

Italy can be called into doubt. The territories of the empire provided vast supplies of manpower and resources – men who could be citizens, soldiers, senators and ultimately emperors, and goods and food in abundance to supply the population. Gradually many of the differences between Italy and the other provinces may have been eroded. Goodman (pp.194–5) summarizes some of the changes which may have confronted Italy and suggests that it may have suffered from economic decline. This, however, is difficult to document and, as the last section illustrated, aspects of the economy appeared to be booming. Despite the richness of evidence for the Roman period in Italy, many issues are unresolved. Uncertainties remain about the interrelationship of the administration, government and economy of Rome and Italy and how these things changed across time (Millar, 1986).

This block has used a wide range of evidence to explore the relationship between Rome and Italy and how the empire affected this relationship. The use of diverse sources – literature, archaeology, architecture, inscriptions, portraiture and so forth – represents the multi-disciplinary approach that is essential in studying the Roman world. Many issues raised in this block will reoccur in the remaining blocks of the course as you explore the relationship between Rome and the provinces. In particular, questions concerning the definition of Roman culture, identity and power and how these impacted on the provinces will surface again and again. How did the inhabitants of the empire define themselves? Was being Roman a matter of accepting Roman power, holding citizenship and living in a Roman-style settlement? Did other identities coexist with or eclipse Roman identity? How is Roman culture to be defined and to what degree can it be differentiated from local, native cultures? It is hoped that the study of Italy in this block has provided some pointers to how these issues should be addressed.

Key dates

Part One

BC	264–241	First Punic War
	225–222	Conquest of Gallia Cisalpina
	218	Foundation of colonies at Piacenza, Cremona and Mantova
	218–202	Second Punic War
	91–87	Social War
	31	Battle of Actium
	25	Conquest of the Salassi and foundation of Aosta
	25–15	Expansion of Gallia Cisalpina
	9–8	Construction of the arch at Susa
	7–6	Augustus decrees the building of the Tropaeum Alpium
	6	Augustus reorganizes the administration of Italy into eleven regions
AD	46	Claudius issues edict concerning citizenship in the municipality of Tridentum
	63	Death of king Cottius II of Susa

Part Two

BC	80	Settlement of Roman colonists in Pompeii
	29	Dedication of the Forum of Julius Caesar
		Dedication of the temple to Julius Caesar in the Forum Romanum
		Dedication of the *curia* in the Forum Romanum
	2	Dedication of the Forum of Augustus
AD	10	Dedication of the temple of Concordia Augusta in the Forum Romanum
	12	Dedication of the Basilica Iulia in the Forum Romanum
	41–54	Reign of Claudius
		New harbour works at Ostia
	59	Riot in Pompeii
	62	Earthquake in Pompeii
	79	The eruption of Vesuvius and destruction of Pompeii
	98–117	Reign of Trajan
		New harbour constructed near Ostia
	112	Dedication of Trajan's Forum

References

BEARD, M. and CRAWFORD, M. (1989) *Rome in the Late Republic*, London, Duckworth.

BRAUND, S. (1988) *Beyond Anger: a Study of Juvenal's Third Book of Satires*, Cambridge, Cambridge University Press.

CRAWFORD, M. (1991) 'Early Rome and Italy' in J. Boardman, J. Griffin and O. Murray (eds) *The Oxford History of the Roman World*, Oxford, Oxford University Press, pp.13–49.

DOBBINS, J.J. (1994) 'Problems of chronology, decoration and urban design in the forum of Pompeii', *American Journal of Archaeology*, vol.98, no.4, pp.629–94.

ETIENNE, R. (1992) *Pompeii: the Day the City Died*, London, Thames and Hudson/ New Horizon.

FELTON, K. and LEE, K.H. (1972) 'The theme of Juvenal's eleventh satire', *Latomus*, vol.31, no.2, pp.1041–6.

JASHEMSKI, W.M.F. (1979) *The Gardens of Pompeii: Herculaneum and the Villas Destroyed by Vesuvius*, New Rochelle, N.Y., Caratzas Brothers.

JONES, F.M.H. (1990) 'The persona and the addressee in Juvenal *Satire* 11', *Ramus, Critical Studies in Greek and Roman Literature*, vol.19, no.2, pp.160–8.

JONGMAN, W. (1988) *The Economy and Society of Pompeii*, Amsterdam, J.C. Gieben.

LAURENCE, R. (1994) *Roman Pompeii*, London and New York, Routledge.

MEIGGS, R. (1973) *Roman Ostia* (second edition), Oxford, Clarendon Press.

MILLAR, F. (1986) 'Italy and the Roman empire: Augustus to Constantine', *Phoenix*, vol.40, pp.295–318.

RADICE, B. (trans.) (1963) *The Letters of the Younger Pliny* (reprinted 1983), Harmondsworth, Penguin Books.

REEKMANS, T. (1971) 'Juvenal's views on social change', *Ancient Society*, vol.2, pp.117–61.

RICHARDSON, L. (1988) *Pompeii, an Architectural History*, Baltimore, John Hopkins University Press.

WALLACE-HADRILL, A. (1994) *Houses and Society in Pompeii and Herculaneum*, Princeton, Princeton University Press.

WEISINGER, K. (1972) 'Irony and moderation in Juvenal XI', *University of California Studies*, vol.5, pp.227–40.

ZANKER, P. (1998) *Pompeii: Public and Private Life* (trans. D. Schneider), Cambridge, Mass., Harvard University Press.

Further reading

The following books are not part of the course materials. You are not expected to obtain, read or study these items. However if you would like to find out more about some of the topics presented in this block you may find the following list a useful starting point.

Primary sources

Juvenal, *The Sixteen Satires.* Suggested translation: P. Green (1974) *Juvenal: the Sixteen Satires* (fourth edition), Harmondsworth, Penguin Classics.

Secondary sources

ETIENNE, R. (1992) *Pompeii: the Day a City Died,* London, Thames and Hudson/New Horizons.

GARNSEY, P. and SALLER, R. (1987) *The Roman Empire: Economy, Society and Culture,* London, Duckworth.

MEIGGS, R. (1973) *Roman Ostia* (second edition), Oxford, Clarendon Press.

POTTER, T.W. (1987) *Roman Italy,* London, Guild Publishing.

ZANKER, P. (1998) *Pompeii: Public and Private Life* (trans. D. Schneider), Cambridge, Mass., Harvard University Press.